THE MANTLE

Lessons in the Anointing from the Life of Elisha

Tim Decker

Timothy R. Decker, Publisher

ISBN 978-0-6151-3918-0

timothyrdecker@gmail.com

www.lulu.com

ACKNOWLEDGEMENTS

My deep gratitude to Gary Nielsen for sharing the anointing, for his vision and faithful intercession on behalf of my ministry—and my writing this book in particular, and for his relentless encouragement.

My thanks to Y. Sisir Bhushan of India for first suggesting that I write on this theme.

My thanks to Carol Waite for proofreading, to my daughter Sylvia for proofreading and formatting the text and for the cover photograph and design, to my daughter Mary for her work in designing the cover, and to my wife Jan for proofreading and coordinating the Scripture quotations and for her endless support of my writing.

And thanks to all the others whose prayers and appreciation of my ministry have helped me along the way.

CONTENTS

1

THE ANOINTING

The meaning of anointing

Even where anointing is mentioned in the story of Elisha, it does not quite mean what I intend by it here, so I need to explain why I use the term at all.

The usual Old Testament meaning of anointing is literally to apply oil—especially for ritual purposes. God's instructions to Moses about the system of worship for Israel include a recipe of various spices for anointing oil (Exodus 30:23-33):

> *Take for yourself quality spices...and you shall make from these a holy anointing oil...with it you shall anoint the tabernacle of meeting and the ark of the testimony; the table...the lampstand...and the altar of incense; the altar of burnt offering...and the laver.... You shall consecrate them, that they may be most holy.... And you shall anoint Aaron and his sons, and consecrate them.... And you shall speak to the children of Israel, saying, "This shall be a holy anointing oil to Me throughout your generations."*

The purpose of the anointing is to consecrate and make holy—that is, to set apart for God's use. People and objects could be marked for special holy purpose by the rite of anointing.

The method of anointing is graphically described in the psalmist's account of the anointing of Aaron, setting him apart for the priesthood (Psalm 133:2):

> *It is like the precious oil upon the head, running down on the beard, the beard of Aaron, running down on the edge of his garments.*

This is no polite little gesture—the oil is poured out in abundance and covers the person's head, and drips all over the clothing. The one anointed has no doubt about the experience, and the application of oil is obvious as well to others looking on.

Later, when the first kings of Israel are anointed—and whether the oil is made of the recipe given to Moses is hard to say—we get a little closer to the meaning I want to use. Saul is anointed by Samuel (I Samuel 10:1):

> *Then Samuel took a flask of oil and poured it on his head, and kissed him and said, "Is it not because the LORD has anointed you commander over His inheritance?"*

After Samuel anoints Saul, he tells him to expect an encounter with a group of prophets, and he says (I Samuel 10:6),

> *Then the Spirit of the LORD will come upon you and you will prophesy with them and be turned into another man.*

Verse 9 relates:

> *So it was, when he had turned his back to go from Samuel, that God gave him another heart..*

The anointing with oil is first followed by a change of heart, and further (v. 10,11),

> *When they came there to the hill, there was a group of prophets to meet him; then the Spirit of God came upon him, and he prophesied among them.*

Later, when the kingdom is taken from Saul because of his disobedience, David is anointed to replace him as king (I Samuel 16:13):

> *Then Samuel took the horn of oil and anointed him in the midst of his brothers; and the Spirit of the LORD came upon David from that day forward.*

In each case, a man is marked for a special purpose and vested with authority by the application of oil. What happens next—for both Saul and David—gives more of a hint of the important meaning I adopt: in these Old Testament accounts, anointing with literal oil triggers a release of the Holy Spirit. Later, anointing—originally a term for the application of special oil as a mark of consecration—becomes for Isaiah a direct term for an infusion of the power of the Holy Spirit.

When Isaiah says (Isaiah 61:1),

> *The Spirit of the Lord GOD is upon me, because the LORD has anointed me,*

he gives us the bridge into the more common New Testament meaning of anointing.

This passage from Isaiah becomes the manifesto of Jesus of Nazareth as He begins His ministry. Jesus, Luke tells us, returns from His baptism and wilderness temptation (Luke 4:14)

> *in the power of the Spirit to Galilee.*

Jesus Himself explains this power by reading publicly from the prophecy of Isaiah (Luke 4:18,19):

> *The Spirit of the LORD is upon Me, because He has anointed Me to preach the gospel to the poor; He has sent Me to heal the brokenhearted, to proclaim liberty to the captives and recovery of sight to the blind, to set at liberty those who are oppressed, to proclaim the acceptable year of the LORD.*

The phrases, "the Spirit of the Lord is upon" and "He anointed" clearly mean the same thing, bringing together the term anointing with the meaning of the applied power of the Holy Spirit.

Peter says of Jesus' ministry (Acts 10:38),

> *God anointed Jesus of Nazareth with the Holy Spirit and with power, who went about doing good and healing all who were oppressed by the devil, for God was with Him.*

John uses the term in his first epistle when he says of believers generally (I John 2:20,27),

> *But you have an anointing from the Holy One...the anointing which you have received from Him abides in you, and you do not need that anyone teach you; but as the same anointing teaches you concerning all things, and is true, and is not a lie, and just as it has taught you, you will abide in Him.*

John is saying that we have an anointing which not only teaches us, but also puts us in close contact with the Holy One.

This contact with the Holy Spirit can thus be described by a one-word term that we can use as a kind of spiritual shorthand. If we want to talk about contact with God, or what we sense as a revelation of God, or God working through us to affect other people or to influence circumstances, we can call it the *anointing*. And this is what I mean by offering lessons in the anointing from the life and ministry of Elisha.

The Holy Spirit as a Person

We need to ask, Is the Holy Spirit a Person—what we call the third Person of the Trinity—or is the Holy Spirit a substance, like oil, that can be poured out and applied?

The traditional and orthodox answer is that the Holy Spirit is a Person. The Bible doesn't use the term *Person* to describe the Holy Spirit, but the meaning is there by implication. Jesus, in describing the ministry of the Holy Spirit, clearly uses personal pronouns—*He* and *Him* and *whom* (John 14:16-17,26):

> *"And I will pray the Father, and He will give you another Helper, that He may abide with you forever–the Spirit of truth, whom the world cannot receive, because it neither sees Him nor knows Him; but you know Him, for He dwells with you, and will be in you…the Helper, the Holy Spirit, whom the Father will send in My name, He will teach you."*

And (John 16:13,14):

> *"However, when He, the Spirit of truth, has come, He will guide you into all truth; for He will not speak on His own authority, but whatever He hears, He will speak; and He will tell you things to come. He will glorify Me, for He will take of what is Mine and declare it to you."*

Not only once, but over and over, Jesus refers to the Holy Spirit as to a Person. The importance of this is to inform us of a personal relationship: the revelation and the help that we receive come from the heart of God. When the Holy Spirit helps us, it is not good luck or fate that we have to thank, but rather the Lover of our souls who is intimately concerned with everything about us. When we have insight into truth, it is not a cosmic consciousness we are tapping into by means of a sensitive intuition, but it is the Teacher who is guiding us to know Himself and His ways.

This personal relationship is at the core of what sets Christianity apart from all the religions of the world. We are not simply honoring a myth, or following doctrine and ritual, or engaging power; we are falling in love. All the notable Christians about whom books are written to inspire others seem to have this in common—that they are passionate about Jesus. They have learned to trust the voice of His Spirit guiding their decisions, encouraging them in difficulty, and taking them to deeper levels of understanding.

The Holy Spirit as a substance

But for all the scriptural evidence of a personal Holy Spirit, this difficulty arises: there are also many scriptures describing the Holy Spirit as a substance. The fact that we can discuss the anointing means that there is something about the Holy Spirit very like oil—or ointment—that can be poured on us.

In the wonderful story—repeated in three Gospels—of the woman healed of the flow of blood, Jesus reveals that His healing power is something that He can actually feel as it moves from Himself to the sick (Luke 8:43-46):

> *Now a woman, having a flow of blood for twelve years…came from behind and touched the border of His garment. And immediately her flow of blood stopped. And Jesus said, "Who touched Me?" …Peter…said, "Master, the multitudes throng and press You, and You say, 'Who touched Me?'" But Jesus said, "Somebody touched Me, for I perceived power going out from Me."*

The anointing flows, not in a figurative sense, but as a tangible substance. It almost seems to be like electrical current. But it is

11

unlike electricity in that the release of power is activated not alone by the woman touching Jesus' clothes, but in combination with her faith. The passage makes plain that others touch Jesus without a flow of the anointing. What makes the woman's touch different is her faith, as Jesus confirms (v. 48),

> *And He said to her, "Daughter…your faith has made you well."*

Her faith triggers the anointing, and a discernable flow of the Holy Spirit not only causes her body to be healed but also allows Jesus to sense the rush of power.

At Pentecost, Peter explains to the people in Jerusalem that the phenomenal effect on the 120 believers is due to (Acts 2:16,17)

> *"what was spoken by the prophet Joel: 'And it shall come to pass in the last days,' says God, 'that I will pour out of My Spirit on all flesh.'"*

This point is followed up later in Peter's address when he says of the resurrected Christ (v. 33),

> *"Therefore being exalted to the right hand of God, and having received from the Father the promise of the Holy Spirit, He poured out this which you now see and hear."*

The fact is the Holy Spirit is pourable—as strange as this may seem.

When Jesus speaks with the woman at the well of Sychar in Samaria, He tells her that He has better water to give her than what she can give Him from the well (John 4:10,14):

> *Jesus answered and said to her, "If you knew the gift of God, and who it is who says to you, 'Give Me a drink,' you would have asked Him, and He would have given you living water…. Whoever drinks of the water that I shall give him will never thirst. But the water that I shall give him will become in him a fountain of water springing up into everlasting life."*

In this story we are left to guess what Jesus means by "living water." But later, at a Jewish feast in Jerusalem, Jesus (John 7:37,38)

> *cried out, saying, "If anyone thirsts, let him come to Me and drink. He who believes in Me, as the Scripture has said, out of his heart will flow rivers of living water."*

This time John adds the explanation (v.39),

> *But this He spoke concerning the Spirit, whom those believing in Him would receive.*

Now we see that when Jesus speaks of living water He means the Holy Spirit. We are given to believe that there is about the Holy Spirit a characteristic understood by what we know of water. Water flows—like oil—and you can pour it, but you can also drink it. Evidently the Holy Spirit is like that.

Paul describes the Holy Spirit in water-like terms (I Corinthians 12:13):

> *For by one Spirit we were all baptized into one body...and have all been made to drink into one Spirit.*

Here the picture is again of drinking—that is, taking the Holy Spirit inside us. But also there is the picture of baptism—or of immersion or soaking in the Holy Spirit. The root meaning of baptism is to dip—as cloth into a dye; the cloth takes on the identity of the dye by permanently sharing its color. Somehow, literal water baptism and baptism in the Holy Spirit are linked. Visible, physical water baptism is the initiating act of faith by which we are identified with Christ and His church. But there is also an invisible inner baptism by which our spirit is dipped into the Spirit of Christ and takes on an identity as part of His spiritual body. (I assume that when Paul says, in Ephesians 4:5, there is

> *"one baptism"*

he means that these two phases—both outer and inner baptism—are but the one union with Christ that all believers are brought into by faith.) At any rate, the Holy Spirit is both living water that is in us, and living water that we are in.

A wonderful description of living water comes to us in Ezekiel's vision of water flowing from the temple. In the vision, the water becomes a river that gets deeper and deeper, bringing life to all in its path (Ezekiel 47:1-12):

> *And there was water, flowing from under the threshold of the temple...; the water was flowing from...south of the altar. ...he measured one thousand cubits, and he brought me through the waters; the water came up to my ankles. Again he measured one thousand and brought me through the waters; the water came up to my knees. Again...the water came up to my waist. Again...it was a river that I could not cross; for the water was too deep, water in which one must swim.... Then he said to me:... "And it shall be that every living thing that moves, wherever the rivers go, will live. ...Along the bank of the river...will grow all kinds of trees.... Their fruit will be for food, and their leaves for medicine."*

When we compare this description with what John sees in the Revelation, we notice that the rivers are likely one and the same (Revelation 22:1,2):

> *And he showed me a pure river of water of life, clear as crystal, proceeding from the throne of God and of the Lamb. ...and on either side of the river, was the tree of life, which bore twelve fruits.... And the leaves of the tree were for the healing of the nations.*

If we remember that John tells us that the living water is the Holy Spirit, we have a magnificent picture of the Holy Spirit's life-giving power, but also of His river-like flow, endless and abundant— enough to swim in. Besides the characteristics of oil and water, Paul also mentions another form of liquid that is like the Holy Spirit when he says (Ephesians 5:18),

> *And do not be drunk with wine...but be filled with the Spirit.*

It is a little more difficult to accept that the fullness of the Holy Spirit could be compared in any way to wine and the effects of alcohol. But before we dismiss the possibility, let's remember that on Pentecost people who had encountered the Holy Spirit were thought to be drunk (Acts 2:15):

> *"These are not drunk, as you suppose."*

To a conservative mind, the thought of being so overwhelmed by the anointing of the Holy Spirit that we might lose control in merriment and staggering seems irreverent if not impossible. But if we consider that not only is there biblical precedent—the 120 at Pentecost—there may be, as well, a reasonable explanation. On the one hand, there is the vast power of our infinite God, and, on the other hand, the fragility of human nature. Is it not a wonder that mankind can at all be touched by—let alone be filled with and immersed in—the Holy Spirit without being destroyed altogether in some sort of physical and/or emotional melt-down? Why should a dizzying reaction be improbable?

In addition to oil, water, and wine, the Holy Spirit is likened also to wind. Playing on the meaning of the word for spirit in Greek that is the same as the word for wind (*pneuma*), and in Hebrew the same as the word for breath (*ruach*), Jesus says (John 3:6,8),

> *That which is born of the flesh is flesh, and that which is born of the Spirit [wind] is spirit [wind]... The wind [Spirit] blows where it wishes and you hear the sound of it, but cannot tell where it comes from and where it goes. So is everyone who is born of the Spirit [wind].*

Returning to Ezekiel, we see in the vision of the valley of the dry bones that the bones come together and are covered with flesh yet do not live until (Ezekiel 37:9,10)

> *He said to me, "Prophesy to the breath, prophesy, son of man, and say to the breath, 'Thus says the Lord GOD, "Come from the four winds, O breath, and breathe on these slain, that they may live."'" So I prophesied as He commanded me, and breath came into them, and they lived, and stood upon their feet, an exceedingly great army.*

Wind is not actually a substance, of course, but it does involve the substance of air, and it has tangible force and sound. All of this is underscored at Pentecost when (Acts 2:2-4)

> *Suddenly there came a sound from Heaven as of a rushing*

15

mighty wind, and it filled the whole house where they were sitting… And they were all filled with the Holy Spirit.

The Holy Spirit as a Person and as a substance

Which is it then? Is the Holy Spirit a Person, or is the Holy Spirit a substance? Given the many examples from Scripture, I think we would do best to conclude that the Holy Spirit is both. Paul, in a single verse of Scripture, combines the concepts of personal love and pourable substance when he says (Romans 5:5),

> *The love of God has been poured out in our hearts by the Holy Spirit who was given to us.*

And if we ask, "How can a Person also be a substance like oil, water, wine, and wind?" part of the answer—and perhaps the most important part—might be to consider whether God's existence is limited to a logical definition.

We think of a person in human terms, and that means having a mind, will, and emotions—a personality—contained, more or less, in a body. I can walk up to someone, hold out my hand, and say, "How do you do? I am Tim Decker." The other person can look at me and see my physical dimensions, catch an impression from my face and my voice, and observe the clothing I wear and how I move. As we talk, their perception of my personality develops. They have met Tim Decker.

They could also visit a river, and swim in it, or, under the right conditions, drink from it. They could apply various lotions to their body. Or they could feel a gentle breeze—or a threatening hurricane.

However, if we should meet again and I were to say, "I flow as a river, and I am applied as lotion, and I blow as the wind," they would properly think me mad. They might reply, "I recognize you as the person I met the other day, but it is impossible that you are a river." This is because humanity has finite limits, and human persons are defined in a limited way.

But why should we think that God's existence is limited to a definition like ours? Who is to say what are the limitations of the eternal, infinite, Creator Spirit—especially when, in His written Word, He refers to so many substance-like ways of relating? If it is fitting to say (Ephesians 4:30),

Do not grieve the Holy Spirit of God,

indicating an emotional quality of personality, why is it not equally fitting to say (I Thessalonians 5:19),

Do not quench the Spirit,

indicating burning substance?

Perhaps we have a fear that if we allow for substance-like qualities in the Holy Spirit—as distinct from personality traits—we open the door to occult values. After all, flowing energy, auras, karma, and the like are all occult New Age concepts of spiritual substance. One of the more popular movie themes of recent times is the Force of the *Star Wars* series. The Force is an impersonal power that can be invoked for good or evil by those who believe in it. *Star Wars* is really an occult tract (in the form of a movie produced by a confessed occult believer)—popularizing the notion of spiritual power available to all. In what amounts to an occult blessing, characters in the movie say to each other, "The Force be with you."

I actually once saw a bumper sticker adding to the confusion: "The Force is with me. His name is Jesus." It was a clever attempt to relate the gospel to popular culture, but it was off-target by light years. The reason it was off-target is that the New Age concept of impersonal power, called in the movie the Force, is totally different from the very personal and very Holy Spirit of God.

The truth is that there exists a spirit realm in which both good and evil operate. It is helpful to notice that Paul uses the same word, "Heavenlies," or the phrase, "Heavenly places," in Ephesians to describe the location of both good and evil. In the first chapter, Paul says (v.3),

Blessed be the God and Father of our Lord Jesus Christ, who

> *has blessed us with every spiritual blessing in the heavenly*
> *places in Christ.*

Paul continues (v. 20),

> *He raised [Christ] from the dead and seated Him at His right*
> *hand in the heavenly places.*

But in chapter six, in a description of spiritual warfare, Paul identifies the enemy as (v.12)

> *principalities,…powers,…the rulers of the darkness of this*
> *age, …spiritual hosts of wickedness in the heavenly places.*

Occult power is real (God, after all, created the fallen spirits before their rebellion), but it is warped and deceptive—and generally passes itself off as impersonal power. Whether we call it the Force or good vibrations or cosmic energy, all New Age power comes from Satan and is a weak corruption of the power of God. The comfort for God's people is that our God is in control, and that His power is neither impersonal nor relative, but personal and absolute. That is, while the Holy Spirit flows as a powerful substance, the power is unlike the Force of the movies or the "healing touch" of New Agers, because, first, He is not something we use; He uses us. Second, He loves us personally, and His power is not separate from His holy, loving, righteous, wise, compassionate heart.

There may be a measure of fear among some Christians who think that any supernatural power is—or might possibly be—of Satan and therefore to be avoided. And if that were true, anything I have to say about the anointing would be dangerous (even though it is in the Bible), because the anointing has to do with the flow of supernatural power. What such Christians overlook is that we are already involved in the spirit realm whether we like it or not (Ephesians 6:12):

> *For we do not wrestle against flesh and blood, but against*

the forces of evil in "the heavenly places," as we have already seen. We need to embrace rather than avoid the anointing as the means the Holy Spirit uses to make ordinary people into extraordinary saints. When we experience the powerful substance of the anointing flowing on us and in us and through us, we will also find ourselves in love with God and delightedly fulfilling His holy will, overcoming—rather than cooperating with—evil powers.

Elisha and the anointing

I use the term *anointing* in this book about Elisha to describe the manifest presence and applied power of the Holy Spirit of God, despite two features of Elisha's story. One is that anointing with literal oil has a place in the story, and the other is that the power of God is not actually called anointing in this part of Scripture. But anointing in the spiritual sense of the manifest presence and applied power of God—as I have been describing—is useful for my purpose since I am looking from a New Testament point of view.

While all of Scripture is ultimately about the anointing, the story of Elisha holds many specific examples of this supernatural power, told in a way that allows us to see a spectrum of the anointing at work: the variety is balanced; the details are refreshingly apt. The interpretations I offer are not necessarily the only interpretations, but there are lessons about the anointing to be learned, and my observations may help in their discovery.

2

ELIJAH

The calling

Elijah precedes Elisha. His dramatic appearance almost out of nowhere, to confront King Ahab and his pagan queen Jezebel with her prophets of Baal, more or less defines the role of an Old Testament prophet: righteous indignation combines with spiritual authority to call Israel back to Jehovah. But as Elijah's ministry is drawing to a close, God tells him (in I Kings 19) to anoint two new kings—Hazael in Syria and Jehu in Israel—and then to pass on his prophetic ministry by anointing Elisha.

It is interesting that there is no record of Elijah ever actually anointing the kings, though perhaps there is a reason for this that I will mention later. Neither is there an account of the anointing of Elisha—that is, with literal oil—although that may have happened without being recorded. What is recorded is found in I Kings 19:19 and following, and reveals the first principle that I want to point out:

> So he departed from there, and found Elisha the son of Shaphat, who was plowing with twelve yoke of oxen before him, and he was with the twelfth. Then Elijah passed by him and threw his mantle on him. And he left the oxen and ran after Elijah, and said, "Please let me kiss my father and my mother, and then I will follow you." And he said to him, "Go back again, for what have I done
>
> to you?"

Because of this story, receiving "a mantle" has become a symbol of the transfer of position or power. But there is no mention of such a custom anywhere else in Scripture. There is no reason to believe that it was a standard means of one prophet transferring ministry to another. But nevertheless Elisha knows what the mantle is for. How does he know?

The answer, it seems to me, is that some time before this happens Elisha had felt a stirring in his spirit. Perhaps it was as far back as childhood and he had known all his life that there was a calling upon him. Or perhaps it was only recently. It is possible that he understood only vaguely that there was something he was destined to fulfill. Or—and we can only guess at this—he may have had a very clear prophetic word or vision of one day walking in Israel as a prophet of the Most High God. Whatever the background details, we know that Elisha's response to Elijah ("Please let me kiss my father and my mother, and then I will follow you.") is something the senior prophet attempts to dismiss ("What have I done to you?"). In other words, Elijah is saying that the mantle in itself means nothing. But because Elisha responds with understanding, it is evidence of his having heard from God. And the mantle is not so much a summons from Elijah as a signal from the Lord: *This, Elisha, is what you have been waiting for; the power you feel in this mantle confirms the call you have felt in your spirit—get going!*

Moses' sense of calling is another example from the Old Testament. Even before Moses' encounter at the burning bush, he has the stirring in his heart as a prophet of God and as a deliverer of God's people. As a young man he rises up against an Egyptian oppressor and, consequently, as Hebrews 11:27 tells us,

> *By faith he forsook Egypt…for he endured as seeing Him who is invisible.*

When, forty years later, the voice of God speaks from the burning bush to send Moses back to Egypt, it is but a confirmation of the earlier call.

Elisha's calling has a parallel in the New Testament as well. When two men meet together with a group of prophets and teachers in Antioch, a message comes from the Holy Spirit (Acts 13:2),

> *"Now separate to Me Barnabus and Saul [later Paul] for the*

21

work to which I have called them."

The significant phrase here is, *"I have called them."* They have already experienced a call, and what remains is for the Antioch group to confirm the call. The group does not appoint these men as apostles; they simply are led to announce that this is God's time for them to go. Paul makes this clear when he identifies himself as (Galatians 1:1)

> *Paul, an apostle (not from men nor through man, but through Jesus Christ and God the Father, who raised Him from the dead).*

This is true also in the life of Jesus. Long before the public confirmation of His call at His baptism, as a child Jesus knows that He is to (Luke 2:49)

> *"be about My Father's business."*

Whether Old Testament or New, whether prophet or apostle or Christ, the first principle of the anointing is that it is preceded by a call—a stirring of the spirit—and then by a confirmation of the call.

The price of responding to the call

Besides acknowledging that Elijah's thrown mantle confirms a previous call, Elisha himself does something to seal the confirmation (I Kings 19:21):

> *So Elisha turned back from him, and took a yoke of oxen and slaughtered them and boiled their flesh, using the oxen's equipment, and gave it to the people and they ate.*

Response to the call of God means sacrifice. Elisha the farmer is called to a greater field, and the old farm and its ways no longer hold a responsibility for him. The oxen and the yoke and the plow—once the means of livelihood—become to this man of God the stuff of sacrifice as he turns his back forever on life as he has known it.

Responding to God's call is costly and life changing. The

one called can never again fit comfortably in the old ways, and there comes a moment when there is no more looking back. For Elisha it means the sacrifice of the oxen and implements. For Abraham it is forsaking his country and his father's house. When Peter, Andrew, James and John hear Jesus' call (Matthew 4:20,22),

> *They immediately left their nets…the boat and their father, and followed Him.*

Saul of Tarsus faces up to the loss of all the racial pride and religious security of his natural heritage (Philippians 3:5-7, 12):

> *Circumcised the eighth day, of the stock of Israel, of the tribe of Benjamin, a Hebrew of the Hebrews; concerning the law, a Pharisee; concerning zeal, persecuting the church; concerning the righteousness which is in the law, blameless. But what things were gain to me, these I have counted loss for Christ…that I may lay hold of that for which Christ Jesus has also laid hold of me.*

And the Lord Jesus Himself, in pursuit of the call of the Father (Philippians 2:6,7),

> *being in the form of God, did not consider it robbery to be equal with God, but made Himself of no reputation, taking the form of a bond-servant..*

The value of sacrifice

Besides giving him the freedom to pursue the call, another benefit of Elisha's sacrifice of the oxen is that he (I Kings 19:21)

> *gave it to the people and they ate.*

There is about our personal sacrifice something that releases blessing to other people; sacrifice is nourishing to the spirit. Of Jesus, Paul says (II Corinthians 8:9),

> *For you know the grace of our Lord Jesus Christ, that though He was rich, yet for your sakes He became poor, that you through His poverty might become rich.*

And Jesus Himself explains this death-to-life principle in the simple picture of a seed planted (John 12:24):

> *Most assuredly, I say to you, unless a grain of wheat falls into the ground and dies, it remains alone; but if it dies, it produces much grain.*

For Paul, the calling is not simply to a renowned ministry—replete with an anointing seldom if ever equaled. Nor is his sacrifice only the loss of reputation; the Lord informs Ananias about the newly converted Saul (Acts 9:15,16),

> *"He is a chosen vessel of Mine to bear My name before Gentiles, kings, and the children of Israel. For I will show him how many things he must suffer for My name's sake."*

Paul explains this phenomenon when he describes the various forms of suffering through the years of his career that follow, not as so many strokes of bad luck, but as a recipe for blessing others (II Corinthians 4:10-12):

> *always carrying about in the body the dying of the Lord Jesus, that the life of Jesus also may be manifested in our body. For we who live are always delivered to death for Jesus' sake, that the life of Jesus also may be manifested in our mortal flesh. So then death is working in us, but life in you.*

Beware the supposed call to an anointed ministry that does not involve sacrifice! It is those who pass through the fire who have gold to give; it is those who fall into the earth and die who produce a harvest; and it is those who slay the oxen who can feed the people.

Following the leader

Without the call and without the sacrifice there can be no hope of successful pursuit of the anointing. But there remains another principle, sometimes little understood but powerful when experienced, shown in the final sentence of this opening passage (I Kings 19:21):

> *Then he arose and followed Elijah, and became his servant.*

What grace comes upon the relationship of spiritual mentoring! The aging prophet, full of years and experience, allows the younger man to be with him as he lives his prophetic life in the anointing. It doesn't say about these two that there is an overt teaching mode involved. In fact, the wording suggests that Elijah is passive; he doesn't have to do anything; he just is himself. But Elisha—in his hunger for the anointing—does what needs to be done: he follows.

How many young prophets, or those with any call of God upon them, would wisely heed Elisha's example! Rather than rush headlong into ministry over-confident in his calling, Elisha seems instinctively to understand that if it is the anointing he wants, he must seek it from a viable source. I once heard an old preacher say, "The anointing is like the measles; you have to be around people who have got it to get it." And how many mature servants of God would do well to encourage younger ones to share in their anointing.

Every mentoring arrangement looks different, because the context is different, the people are different, and the degree of closeness in the relationship is different. And since there are no rules for how mentoring is to be carried out, the arrangement may be long- or short-lived, the parties may be aware of what is happening or oblivious, and the learning process may be intense or incidental.

Probably the most effective mentoring involves a close personal relationship with frequent contact, and—ideally—an acknowledged commitment and affection. But other forms of mentoring work more or less well.

Some of the spiritual mentoring I have received has actually been simply through the writings of godly men. One author who has touched my spirit has had such an impact that, though I had never heard him in person, another older leader who had known the author once told me that when I preached I reminded him of my hero. A heady moment that was for me!

I think of another example. I have over my desk a photograph (taken at my request by my daughter Mary) of the memorial statue of Phillips Brooks. He is best known as the writer of the beloved Christmas carol, "O Little Town of Bethlehem," composed during his pastorate in Philadelphia. But later in life he returned to the city of his birth—Boston. There he flourished in ministry at Trinity Church in Copley Square. The memorial is on a small plaza outside the church and consists of an inscribed marble arch within which stands, in life-size bronze, Phillips Brooks at his pulpit. He is gazing at the congregation before him, one hand on the Bible and the other raised in a preaching gesture. What makes the statue impressive to me is that behind Brooks—also in bronze and larger than life—stands the robed figure of Jesus, also gazing at the congregation, with his right hand resting on the preacher's shoulder.

This bronze pair—the Christian preacher overshadowed and empowered by the Christ—has influenced me since my childhood in Boston. I sometimes would accompany my father, also a pastor, when he took visitors from out of town on a tour of Boston sights. A frequent stop on such tours was Trinity Church and the Brooks memorial. I can remember being fascinated by the thought of the presence of Jesus behind the preacher, with His hand on the man's shoulder as he spoke. Now a preacher myself, I realize that I was being mentored for years by Phillips Brooks, a man whose ministry was empowered by the presence of the Lord Jesus Christ—although my mentor died years before I was born and I knew him only through a statue! (There is a sense in which my father, as well, was mentor in this connection: he modeled for me an appreciation of the godly Brooks—and the anointing hand of Jesus on his ministry.)

And speaking of my father, I need to mention how he has mentored me throughout my life in one particular way: he has passed on to me books that he has read that he has felt would be useful to me as well. I suppose he has given me fifteen or twenty books this way (besides the general bulk of his considerable library that has always been available to me). Most of the books have been timely and helpful personally and in ministry.

Another mentor in my childhood briefly touched my life

when he was on extended furlough as a missionary and led a congregation in a nearby city for a couple of years. Oscar Jacobson knew my father, and more than once he preached in our church and sometimes visited in our home. He would tell hilarious jokes on the one hand, and stories of spiritual warfare from the mission field on the other, in a refreshing mix of godly spontaneity that I sensed was genuine. I can remember hoping I could be like him when I grew up. He won my admiration forever when my father complimented him one day on his new car. "Not mine," Jacobson replied, taking keys out of his pocket and extending them, jingling, towards my father. "The car is yours whenever you want it."

A brief conversation overheard in a Sunday School room qualifies as another bona fide mentoring example from my childhood. Edna White was a professional Christian children's worker; she had run a children's mission in the Boston area for many years. I knew her as a sweet and jolly older woman who liked kids. The scenario was that Miss White was also a Sunday school teacher in our church, but classes were being rearranged in such a way that she would no longer have a class. One Sunday morning I overheard the Sunday school superintendent laboring through a tactful explanation of the reasons for the professional children's worker being bumped out of a Sunday School job. But when Miss White understood where the conversation was going, she interrupted with a laugh. "Oh, you don't have to worry about hurting my feelings, honey," she said. "I died twenty years ago!" What humility! What an example of being crucified with Christ that I have never forgotten!

I was blessed with a more obvious and traditional mentor in Jim Grumbine, an older pastor in nearby Allentown, Pennsylvania, when I was young in ministry. He opened up to me the spiritual realm in a practical way when he invited me to participate with him in deliverance sessions with a person in his church who was clearly troubled. I had believed theoretically in the reality of demons, but I saw with my own eyes manifestations of evil—and of God's overcoming power—as we went through hours of confrontation. What I appreciated most about Jim was the non-aggressive way he shared things related to deliverance and other matters of the Spirit. He never tried to persuade me to believe or experience what he believed and experienced. But he was always ready to answer my questions and to patiently absorb my objections. He never argued; instead he let me work through my issues, as I would probe my own thoughts and then come back to him for his responses. Although we had no formal mentoring relationship, his heart and his method were of the classic mentor: he was available; he shared his heart; he let me be myself; and he modeled practical ministry.

This is likely the sort of way Elijah relates to Elisha—the older mentor showing the ropes to the young recruit. Some things can be learned only by watching another. This is true in almost any field—carpentry, medicine, hunting, counseling, and so forth. There are techniques to practice, disciplines to adopt, and difficulties to overcome that are not taught verbally so much as modeled. Elisha knows that if he is called to prophetic ministry, spending time with a prophet is the best preparation.

When Jesus calls his disciples, there is an order in how He proceeds (Mark 3:14):

> *Then He appointed twelve, that they might be with Him and that He might send them out to preach.*

Before they are sent out, they are to "be with." This is what traditional mentoring is all about: disciples being with a master. The disciples are with Jesus—the Master—when He teaches about the Kingdom, with Him when He heals bodies and casts out demons, with Him when He raises the dead, and some are with Him when He is transfigured. Who can set a value on this kind of learning?

But they are also with Him in off-hours—while walking or riding in a boat or eating. They are with Him in real-life settings; and that means that besides learning how to work the crowds, they learn how to live. In the camaraderie of His presence, they experience godliness in ordinary situations. The effectiveness of a mentor—and a spiritual mentor in particular—is not in being superhuman, beyond reach. Sound mentoring means modeling extraordinary life in the context of ordinary living.

Something else happens that is a vital part of spiritual mentoring (Matthew 10:1):

> *He gave them power over unclean spirits, to cast them out, and to heal all kinds of sickness and all kinds of disease.*

Another term for power is *anointing*. The Twelve receive an impartation of the Holy Spirit's anointing to do the supernatural Kingdom ministry for which Jesus sends them. Followers learn by the example of a mentor, but this miraculous power is on a different level, and it emphasizes the value of "being with" in a different way. It helps us define the anointing as a transferable phenomenon that is received in close association.

A godly mentor always imparts to a learner more than wisdom and technique. Beyond what can be seen naturally on the outside, something happens in the unseen spiritual realm: the anointing is shared and transferred by simple association as well as by the more direct means of laying on hands and prayer ministry. The mentor shares spiritual DNA with the learner that becomes a more or less permanent resource. There are variables that influence how much anointing is transferred, of course—such variables as the degree of anointing on the mentor, the receptivity of the learner, and, above all, the providence of God. But while nothing about the anointing can be exactly calculated, the principle remains that the power of the Holy Spirit tends to flow from one person to another and more so in close association.

The role of a servant

A final observation in this study of Elisha's call, especially his response to the call in following Elijah, is that the younger man (I Kings 19:21)

> *became his servant.*

Elisha understands that the best way to learn from the senior prophet is not only to spend time with him, but to serve him. In a culture such as ours in 21st Century America, being a servant is not generally valued. The value might be enhanced, depending on the social status of the one served (for example, someone extremely wealthy, powerful or famous), or in the case of impressive financial reward. But serving an old man, both poor and fugitive, might seem a bad idea.

Why, then, does Elisha serve Elijah?

Perhaps there are several reasons. First, he understands—as we generally don't—that young men ought to do the work (Lamentations 3:27):

> *It is good for a man to bear the yoke in his youth.*

Second, youth ought to defer to age (Leviticus 19:32):

> *You shall rise before the gray headed and honor the presence of an old man.*

Third, humble service is the path to greatness (Matthew 23, 11,12):

> *But he who is greatest among you shall be your servant. And whoever exalts himself will be abased, and he who humbles himself will be exalted.*

Fourth, righteous reward is appropriate. Paul teaches that those ministered to in the Spirit owe those who minister (I Corinthians 9:11):

> *If we have sown spiritual things for you, is it a great thing if we should reap your material things?*

And finally, in a way somewhat related but seen from another angle, there is the blessing of giving and receiving. Jesus says (Luke 6:38),

> *Give, and it will be given to you.*

So the godly mentor, in giving wisdom and encouragement—and anointing, can expect to be given a return from the disciple; and the disciple in serving can expect that an investment of service to the mentor will pay off all the more in dividends of spiritual blessing. The economic advice, "You get what you pay for," is good spiritual advice, as well.

I wish I could say that I had fulfilled the principle of rewarding my mentors. But, as I have said, much of the mentoring I received went unrecognized at the time; only in hindsight have I seen what it was—and how valuable. For the rest, I trust God and my mentors for forgiveness. And I count on God's own blessing upon those who blessed me.

Pursuing the anointing

The Bible uses simple words to state the principle that to have the anointing, or anything in the Kingdom, we must pursue it. What could be more clear than Jesus' three words, *ask*, *seek*, and *knock*, when He tells us how to get the good gifts of the Holy Spirit? Matthew (7:7) and Luke (11:9) both tell us,

> *Ask, and it will be given to you; seek, and you will find; knock, and it will be opened to you.*

God tells Old Testament Israel much the same thing (Jeremiah 29:12-14):

> *Then you will call upon Me and go and pray to Me, and I will listen to you. And you will seek Me and find Me, when you search for Me with all your heart. I will be found by you.*

By spiritual instinct, Elisha heeds this principle of pursuit. The story told in II Kings 2 is of a man who will not be stopped in his quest for the anointing. The first verse says,

> *The LORD was about to take up Elijah into heaven by a whirlwind.*

The passage also shows that this imminent parting is somewhat common knowledge among the men called the "sons of the prophets," and that Elisha himself knows. So when Elijah says to Elisha (II Kings 2:2),

> *"Stay here, please,"*

Elisha responds with bold determination,

> *"As the LORD lives, and as your soul lives, I will not leave you!"*

What is even more remarkable than Elisha's boldness is that this conversation is repeated three times: Elijah asks to withdraw, and Elisha insists on following.

The lesson here is fairly obvious: treasure the anointing; don't let it get away from you. Or, as David says (Psalm 51:11),

> *Do not cast me away from Your presence, and do not take Your Holy Spirit from me.*

And Simon Peter, speaking for the disciples, replies to Jesus when others have forsaken Him and He asks if they are leaving, too (John 6:68),

> *"Lord, to whom shall we go? You have the words of eternal life."*

For the heart that has experienced the presence and power of God, there is no turning back—or, if there is a turning back, it is a sad and inestimable loss. Elisha is determined not to lose what is so nearly within his grasp, and he is willing to make a nuisance of himself in his pursuit.

Crossing the river

As the story in II Kings 2 continues, Elijah and Elisha come to the Jordan River. With his mantle, Elijah strikes the water and it divides so the two can cross over on dry ground. There are three such stories in the Bible; besides this one about Elisha and Elijah at the Jordan River, there is Israel's crossing of the Red Sea at the great event of the Exodus led by Moses; and there is Israel's crossing of the Jordan as they enter the Promised Land under the leadership of Joshua. These other miraculous crossings had happened centuries before Elijah and Elisha enter history, but there may be a connection.

Each of the crossings of Israel—of the Red Sea and the Jordan—marks a transition. And these transitions are significant because Israel passes not only from one place to another, but from one identity to another. Slaves on one side of the Red Sea, Israel becomes free on the other. Wanderers on one side of the Jordan,

Israel inherits a homeland on the other. There are things both lost and gained in these transitions. Though they gain freedom in crossing the Red Sea, Israel loses the familiar and dependable food of Egypt (Numbers 11:4-6):

> *The children of Israel also wept again and said, "Who will give us meat to eat? We remember the fish which we ate freely in Egypt, the cucumbers, the melons, the leeks, the onions, and the garlic; but now our whole being is dried up; there is nothing at all except this manna before our eyes!"*

And although the wilderness wandering of a generation ends when Israel crosses the Jordan into Canaan, what they face in the new territory is a seemingly endless war of conquest. What they gain in real estate, they lose in carefree ease.

For Elisha, the crossing of the Jordan also means a new identity; he crosses over as a disciple of the man of God; but he returns as the man of God in his own right. And as with Israel, in this new status Elisha gains something and loses something. He gains respect and prophetic credibility, but he finds he now has to deal with people and circumstances on his own; he can no longer depend on Elijah's counsel and prophetic words from the Lord.

The double portion

When Elisha says for the third time (II Kings 2:6),

> *"As the LORD lives, and as your soul lives, I will not leave you,"*

it becomes evident that his quest for the anointing is unrelenting. So Elijah offers (v.9),

> *"Ask! What may I do for you, before I am taken from you." And Elisha said, "Please let a double portion of your spirit be upon me."*

It is not clear whether this request means that Elisha wants twice as much power as Elijah has had, or whether he is appealing to the law of primogeniture, where the firstborn son inherits the major part of the estate and thus carries on the family name and fortune. (The scripture record shows that, in fact, twice as many miracles are attributed to Elisha as to Elijah.) But in either case, Elisha's request is bold and extravagant: he is greedy for the anointing. And this is as it should be. The anointing is something to be greedy for.

Those who have tasted and seen the goodness of God will want more. With the anointing, the more you have the more you want. Elisha has learned that God's infinite power is to be sought in the extreme.

Elijah's reply reveals yet another principle of the anointing (v.10):

> *So he said, "You have asked a hard thing. Nevertheless, if you see me when I am taken from you, it shall be so for you; but if not, it shall not be so."*

Elijah is not being petty; but rather he is describing a spiritual law: it is the way of the Spirit that He looks for fertile ground. The anointing seeks opportunity to manifest, and that will always be where there is already openness to the presence and power of God. Elijah is saying, in effect, There is no point in hoping for a greater anointing if you don't know how to function on a lesser level.

Jesus describes this principle when He says (Matthew 13:12),

> *"For whoever has, to him more will be given, and he will have abundance; but whoever does not have, even what he has will be taken away from him."*

And so Elisha is to use the level of revelation he already has in order to attain the double portion he seeks. When, in fact, a fiery chariot and horses appear and Elijah (II Kings 2:11,12)

> *went up by a whirlwind into heaven...Elisha saw it and he cried out, "My father, my father, the chariot of Israel and its horsemen!"*

Elisha passes the test and sees into the spirit realm; the promise of the double portion will be fulfilled.

Fathering in the anointing

As Elisha is parted from Elijah, he cries out instinctively for his spiritual father. Although Elijah does not die, he does depart and Elisha feels the loss of his mentor and he is bereft of a father. One of the secrets of the anointing is that it flows best along lines of relationship, and especially a father relationship. What every heart needs is the healing comfort of the Father's love. Rarely in the Old Testament, but prominent in the New, is the understanding of God as our Father. Jesus' model prayer addresses (Matthew 6:9) *"Our Father..."* and we understand the very nature of God to be founded on a Father-Son relationship: Jesus is the (John 3:16) *only begotten Son*. Paul says that from the Heavenly Father (Ephesians 3:15),

> *the whole family in heaven and earth is named.*

And he tells the Corinthians (I. 4:15),

> *in Christ Jesus I have begotten you through the gospel.*

Natural fathering bears the fruit of personality formation. A child with an adequate father relationship matures with confidence and contentment and with normal social and sexual balance. A child with fathering issues—having an absent, neglecting, overbearing, or abusive father—tends to carry into adulthood emotional handicaps that make self-acceptance and relationships a struggle. Mentoring and fathering are very close—and certainly may overlap, but if there is a difference it is in the degree of emotional attachment. A son or daughter is dependent on a father not only for instruction, but also for affirmation, affection and identity.

I think that this is fairly common wisdom, and I don't intend to offer here further discussion to prove it. But if it is true, then two points can be seen: one, spiritual fathering likely can help remedy natural-father shortcomings; and two, it may be just as important to father people in the Spirit in order to develop wholesome spiritual maturity as it is in the natural in order to develop wholesome character and emotional balance. Perhaps much of the shallowness, instability, and error that can be seen

35

among believers today can be traced to a lack of relational nurturing. Blessed are those whose faith is fathered through caring, counsel, example, and affection.

Receiving the blessing

The next few details of the story all point to the way the anointing is to be received.

The first thing Elisha does is to make an end of his former life (II Kings 2:12):

> *And he took hold of his own clothes and tore them into two pieces.*

This is a simple act of removing his garments until he stands naked before the Lord, destroying the garments so that he cannot relapse to his former view of himself. It is akin to what he does in slaughtering the oxen and burning the plow, but it is a more radical step. By the first act, Elisha renounces his old way of life to embrace the new life with the prophet Elijah; by this second act, he renounces his old identity in order to embrace his new identity as a prophet in his own right. Embracing the new identity comes when (v.13)

> *He also took up the mantle of Elijah that had fallen from him, and went back and stood by the bank of the Jordan.*

He must take up the prophetic mantle as an act of faith. What has clothed Elijah is now to clothe Elisha—not automatically, but as he takes it up for himself. This is no time to wallow in a false humility ("How can I ever live up the anointing of Elijah?"), but it is a time to assume the authority of a man of God.

As Elisha stands at the riverbank, he faces a test. He has crossed to this side of the Jordan by the anointing in the hands of Elijah; to return to the other side, he must use the anointing in his own hands. And so (v. 14),

> *He took the mantle of Elijah that had fallen from him, and struck the water, and said, "Where is the LORD God of Elijah?" And when he also had struck the water, it was*

divided this way and that; and Elisha crossed over.

He himself has to begin to use the anointing by striking the water, since the anointing is intended for use. The anointing is not about titles and theory; it is about power flowing. Paul gives a description of the true authority of his ministry by saying (I Thessalonians 1:5),

> *For our gospel did not come to you in word only, but also in power and in the Holy Spirit.*

Relationship—with God and with men

Here are two more thoughts on Elisha receiving the anointing. One is to notice what he says as he strikes the waters (II Kings 2:14):"Where is the LORD God of Elijah?" He does not say, "Where is the power of Elijah?" because the anointing is not an impersonal supernatural force to be tapped into; the anointing is always about the Lord God Himself. The anointing of the Holy Spirit involves a personal relationship with the living and true God Who chooses to reveal Himself to and through men who fear Him. The anointing is holy and reveals a holy God. And Elisha knows that he will not get very far as a true prophet without a revelation of God. As much as he wants the waters to part, he also wants to engage the God known by Elijah, because seeking the anointing without seeking a relationship is a hollow pursuit.

A second thought is this: Elisha does more than divide the waters, he (II Kings 2:14)

> *crossed over.*

That is, his receiving of the anointing is not just for personal amazement, because the anointing is meant for ministry. Elisha does not stay on the side of the Jordan where he has experienced his closest encounter with heaven. He returns to the world of men who need the power of God in their lives. He returns to where the oil of anointing can be shared so that others are touched with the holy, healing presence.

This is surely what Isaiah means, and what Jesus means when He quotes Isaiah (Luke 4:18),

> *The Spirit of the LORD is upon Me, because he has anointed Me to preach the gospel to the poor. He has sent Me to heal the brokenhearted, to preach deliverance to the captives and recovery of sight to the blind, to set at liberty those who are oppressed, to preach the acceptable year of the LORD.*

The anointing brings good news, healing, deliverance, and revelation to those who need it. Receiving the anointing is never an end in itself; we are always to give it away.

3

THE PROPHET

Curses broken—and spoken

It is reported in the last verse of I Kings 16 that in the days of Ahab (v. 34),

> *Hiel of Bethel built Jericho. He laid its foundation with Abiram his firstborn, and with his youngest son Segub he set up its gates, according to the word of the LORD, which He had spoken through Joshua the son of Nun.*

Jericho is under a curse, pronounced generations before by Joshua after the notorious collapse of its walls when Israel had invaded Canaan. Joshua had cursed the firstborn and youngest sons of whoever might dare rebuild the city.

When Elisha, as the new prophet in Israel, visits Jericho in II Kings 2, it has only recently been rebuilt. The curse by Joshua concerns the family of the re-builder—and has been fulfilled in the death of his sons. But problems continue to plague the inhabitants. II Kings 2 does not call it a curse, but the circumstances suggest one (v. 19):

> *Then the men of the city said to Elisha, "Please notice, the situation of this city is pleasant, as my lord sees; but the water is bad, and the land barren."*

Things look good on the surface, but within is death.

Elisha asks for a new jar with salt in it. I take this to represent the anointing; the salt jar is a visible symbol of the invisible power of God. I don't know why it has to be a new jar or why there has to be salt. But it makes as much sense as striking the Jordan with a mantle to part the waters.

One of the lessons we need to learn early on is that the anointing attaches to obedience, rather than to logic. Mary tells the servants at the wedding in Cana, before Jesus says to fill the pots with water and then to draw out wine (John 2:5),

"Whatever He says to you, do it."

It is because they obey that they are privileged to participate in the release of anointing as Jesus performs His first miracle.

To repeat, the issue is not logic, but obedience. It makes no sense to add salt to bad water to make it good, but when the Holy Spirit is motivating the action, the curse of centuries is removed in a moment (II Kings 2:21,22):

> *Then he went out to the source of the water, and cast in the salt there, and said, "Thus says the LORD: 'I have healed this water; from it there shall be no more death or barrenness.'" So the water remains healed to this day.*

In the very next story Elisha himself pronounces a curse with ominous results (II Kings 2:23,24):

> *And he went up from there to Bethel; and as he was going up the road, some youths came from the city and mocked him, and said to him, "Go up, you baldhead! Go up, you baldhead!" So he turned around and looked at them, and pronounced a curse on them in the name of the LORD. And two female bears came out of the woods and mauled forty-two of the youths.*

There are at least two ways of looking at this sad story, and both are sobering. One way is to see the importance of not mocking the anointing—or those who carry it. Partly because anointed people are just people with the idiosyncrasies that make us all different, it is easy to find something to criticize or make fun of. But the anointing is to be respected, and one way to do that is to respect anointed people. I don't mean to say that either genuine good humor or righteous correction involving God's servants is forbidden. But this story serves as a warning that we are to be very careful to avoid expressions of disrespect. By extension, this warning could apply to any of God's people, for all believers possess the anointing in some degree. Of the people of Israel generally David reminds us (I Chronicles 16:21,22/Psalm

105:14,15),

> *He reproved kings for their sakes, saying, "Do not touch My*
> *anointed ones, and do My prophets no harm."*

The other way of looking at the story of Elisha cursing the lads is to see the seriousness of what we speak: the anointing within us empowers our words. We can actually bless people with our words of blessing. The classic blessing in Numbers 6:24-26,

> *"The LORD bless you and keep you;*
>
> *The LORD make His face shine upon you, and be gracious to you;*
>
> *The LORD lift up His countenance upon you,*
>
> *And give you peace,"*

is followed by this guarantee (v. 27):

> *"So they shall put My name on the children of Israel, and I*
> *will bless them."*

But if blessings actually bless, the danger is that likewise curses actually curse. Jesus curses the fig tree and it withers (Matthew 21:19). James warns that we should not curse men (James 3:8-10):

> *But no man can tame the tongue. It is an unruly evil, full of*
> *deadly poison. With it we bless our God and Father, and*
> *with it we curse men, who have been made in the similitude of*
> *God…. My brethren, these things ought not to be so.*

Although Proverbs 26:2 says,

> *A curse without cause [or undeserved] shall not alight,*

it is those for whom we see just cause that we are most ready to curse: "I hope she gets what she deserves!" or "You will get a cold if you go out in this weather without a coat!" or "He'll never amount to anything." Perhaps we do not seriously intend such expressions as curses with any effect. But what if our words have more power than we think? It may be something to consider, if we are to take seriously the anointing deposited within us by the Spirit of God.

On the other hand, cursing what should be cursed—disease

and evil influence of many kinds—may open the door and clear the path for the blessing we seek. Only the Holy Spirit can lead us in using the anointing, and I am not recommending the practice of cursing everything we don't like. But sometimes the anointing may perhaps best be wielded in the form of a curse—a declaration of the destruction of evil.

Music and the release of the anointing

One day three kings consult Elisha as to the outcome of a battle. But rather than speak a prophetic word immediately, Elisha makes a request that reveals something about the connection between music and the anointing; he says (II Kings 3:15,16),

> *"But now bring me a musician." And it happened, when the musician played, that the hand of the LORD came upon him. And he said, "Thus says the LORD...."*

Apparently music can influence the spiritual realm.

David uses this influence when King Saul is troubled by an evil spirit (I Samuel 16:23):

> *David would take a harp and play it with his hand. Then Saul would become refreshed and well, and the distressing spirit would depart from him.*

David, himself a prophet (Acts 2:30), develops musical worship to perhaps a higher level than had ever before been experienced. His prophetic musical genius virtually invents worship as we know it. The Psalms of David repeatedly promote worship in general, and musical worship in particular, in too many instances to cite here. David's worship schedule involves specially appointed musicians and singers (I Chronicles 25:1):

> *David and the captains of the army separated for the service some of the sons of Asaph, of Heman, and of Jeduthun, who should prophesy with harps, stringed instruments, and cymbals.*

These serve in shifts (v. 8-31):

> *Now the first lot...the second...the third...the twenty-fourth,*

which may correspond to the hours of the day and therefore suggest twenty-four hour musical prophetic worship in the presence of God.

Generations after David, Jehoshaphat becomes a great king because he knows God as David had (II Chronicles 17:3-6):

> *Now the LORD was with Jehoshaphat, because he walked in the former ways of his father David.... [He] sought the God of his father, and walked in His commandments.... Therefore the LORD established the kingdom in his hand...and he had riches and honor in abundance.*

When a great army comes against King Jehoshaphat, he knows what to do (II Chronicles 20:20-22):

> *Jehoshaphat stood and said, "Hear me, O Judah and you inhabitants of Jerusalem: Believe in the LORD your God, and you shall be established.... And when he had consulted with the people, he appointed those who should sing to the LORD, and who should praise the beauty of holiness, as they went out before the army and were saying: "Praise the LORD, for His mercy endures forever." Now when they began to sing and to praise, the LORD set ambushes against [the enemy]...and they were defeated.*

Today when God's people gather, music is always an important part of the meeting. And we need to see that, as with Elisha, music actually is a medium for entering the presence of the Lord God. Whether the secret is that music gets God's attention, or ours—or both, we find our connection in the Spirit enhanced with anointed music.

Music styles differ from place to place and from generation to generation, however. And sometimes one group of people may not easily experience the anointing through music used by another group. It is important, therefore, that believers seek a musical "language," as it were, that most readily opens the door into the presence of God for them. North American styles may or may not be adaptable to Latin Americans—and vice versa—not necessarily because the music of one or the other is not anointed, but because the style is unfamiliar and is therefore difficult to enter into. The same might be said of various other international cultural contrasts: African, Chinese, Italian, and so forth, as well as variations within a culture—as Eighteenth Century hymnody, Twentieth Century Pentecostal, or Black Gospel.

This is not to say that any music at all will do. It is only reasonable to point out that some music will encourage worship and fellowship with God, while some, perhaps, will be neutral, and other music may, in fact, encourage a connection with evil. I am not prepared to define what evil music may be, but a simple test might be to see whether a certain type of music is used in demonic rituals or in promoting violence or promiscuity. Some so-called classical music has occult themes revealed in the title. And some seemingly peaceful contemporary music actually may be designed for New Age occult meditation. And some popular music is popular precisely because its throbbing beat encourages sensual reactions.

John Lewandoski, a man whom I had asked to play drums for worship in our congregation, explained this to me. In his younger days, and before his conversion, John had played in nightclubs in New Jersey (and had at one time, in fact, played in the same band with the also-young and yet-unknown Bruce Springsteen). John had not played the drums since his conversion, and wasn't sure if drums and worship could mix. But I pointed out to him that cymbals, at least, are mentioned in Davidic worship, and I suggested he offer up his drumsticks to the Lord, and see what might happen. As it turned out, John's drumming became a powerfully uplifting part of our worship music. But with a qualification:

John told me something I wish every worship drummer could learn. He said, "I know what I did in the night clubs to turn people on sensually. And that is what I avoid doing in worship." He went on to describe how when he plays now in church, he changes the pattern of the beat every couple of bars, because monotonous throbbing is one of the keys to the sensual power of music that is so effective in clubs. This constant changing of the beat obviously requires technical skill and creativity, but it pays off in a purity of motive and execution in leading God's people in worship. John also knew to subordinate his playing to support the singing, rather than to dominate by being loud and flamboyant.

An argument that sometimes is given to defend the use of any and all kinds of music in worship quotes General William Booth. Booth founded the Salvation Army in order to bring the gospel to the masses who never would have attended a traditional church. He is reported to have said (and I cannot verify the quotation—I am only saying that I have heard this reasoning), when defending his use of popular drinking songs reworked with Christian lyrics, "I don't want the devil to have all the best tunes."

While there may well be some crossover tunes from popular culture usable for the Kingdom, we should be careful not to embrace everything the world offers. Israel is warned about the influence of the godless culture around them, and that care should be taken not to imitate it (Deuteronomy 12: 30):

> "Take heed to yourself that you are not ensnared to follow them…and that you do not inquire after their gods, saying, "How did these nations serve their gods? I also will do likewise."

The idea that Christian musicians should be motivated by secular music needs to be tempered by the awareness that some of the ways of "these nations" are actually an abomination to the Lord. Using the music by which they serve their gods of sex and violence and greed may have the potential of importing into the church an anointing—a flow of spiritual power—from the wrong source.

The importance of the role of worship leaders is seen not when we are impressed with their skillful playing and singing (though skill is important), but in the godly spiritual power they wield. When worship leaders pursue the anointing, their sensitivity to the spiritual realm enables them to move a congregation to a level of worship that energizes faith and—more important—pleases the Lord. Without the anointing, worship leaders and congregation alike run the risk of fitting Isaiah's description of empty worship

(29:13), quoted by Jesus in the Gospels (Matthew 15:8):

> *These people draw near to Me with their mouth, and honor Me with their lips, but their heart is far from Me. And in vain they worship Me.*

If worship music without the anointing is in vain, then sometimes, perhaps, the anointing without music can be elusive. Look once again at the scene of Elisha seeking the manifest presence of God (II Kings 3:15):

> *"But now bring me a musician." And it happened, when the musician played, that the hand of the LORD came upon him.*

The two things go hand in hand—the music and the anointing.

Paul points to this holy combination in Ephesians 5:18,19:

> *Be filled with the Spirit, speaking to one another in psalms and hymns and spiritual songs, singing and making melody in your heart to the Lord.*

The Holy Spirit and our own spirit are both attracted to musical worship, and experiencing the fullness of the Spirit is related to experiencing "melody in your heart."

As a small child I experienced the power of anointed music in a way I have never forgotten. I was raised in a denomination known for its missionary zeal, but not for its enthusiastic worship. However, at one summer Bible conference of our district, a guest soloist, Eimer Woermo, a Scandinavian tenor, was engaged to bring what is called special music. And special it was. I can still picture the large tabernacle with many doors opening onto the surrounding lawn, and the wooden benches filled with people—about a thousand of them—gathered for the annual conference. But most of all I remember that when Eimer Woermo sang, something happened that I had never seen before—nor did I see it ever again in the twenty years I remained in that denomination. A few bars into the tenor's song, people began to weep. I can remember as a child being somewhat alarmed at all the weeping, but also in awe. I knew there was something powerful going on. Besides weeping, all over the tabernacle the congregation waved handkerchiefs—hands by the hundreds raised a swaying cloud of white cloth as the singing went blessedly on and on. This phenomenon happened throughout the week of the conference as the presence of the Holy Spirit stirred hearts through the music the tenor sang at each service.

Some might say that this was all meaningless emotionalism, but, as I have pointed out, these people were not used to doing this sort of thing and, to my knowledge, never did it again. There was, therefore, no expectation that emotions should rise when someone sang. And I recall nothing dramatic in the behavior of the soloist to manipulate the crowd to an emotional response. It was a spontaneous reaction to what is best explained as a visitation from God. And a once-small boy has carried into middle age the memory of a place where people were touched, almost unbearably, with the grace of anointed music.

Weeping and waving handkerchiefs is not what the anointing is about, of course. These were only manifestations of something deeper. What anointed music does is bring a sense of the presence of God—revealing His glory and power and love to the human spirit. For Elisha the music releases a prophetic revelation. For the people attending that summer conference half a century ago the music released awe and joy.

When Jesus tells the Samaritan woman at the well of Sychar (John 4:24),

> *God is Spirit and those who worship Him must worship in spirit and truth,*

He is defining something beyond what can be produced naturally. True worship is an anointed experience, meaning that there is an encounter in the realm of the spirit. When music touches our spirit with a revelation of God's presence, true worship results, because we find ourselves in a reality beyond our intellectual perception and, to use Mary's words (Luke 1:46,47),

> *"My soul magnifies the Lord, and my spirit has rejoiced in God my Savior."*

Further, this worship with music in spirit and truth is

47

independent of the musical form used. A pipe organ playing traditional hymns or a guitar playing contemporary songs are equally suitable to a release of the anointing. Likewise, neither form guarantees the anointing. What counts is for the worshipers to experience the presence of the exalted Lord with joy.

The phenomenon known as contemporary worship now used by many churches—sometimes in a separate service for younger people—likely copies an upbeat musical style arising from the charismatic movement. The charismatics of the 1970s and '80s experienced a degree of anointing in their worship—breaking out of tradition and into the presence of God with a new kind of music that produced joy and passion. And many outside their theological circles recognized the life that flowed as they played and sang and clapped their hands.

I have already suggested that a culturally appropriate musical "language" makes worship easier for a congregation. But when a contemporary music style is imitated without the anointing of the Holy Spirit, the result may be closer to a sing-along or a concert than to worship. A sad counterfeit of worship results when the music is designed to attract a certain group of people so that church attendance may increase. The music needs rather to encourage an increase in the flow of the anointing. True, the music style must be something the worshippers can embrace rather than reject, but the style is not an end in itself. The hearts of the composers and musicians need to be more in touch with God than with either tradition or trends, in order to provide an anointed atmosphere in which worship is supernaturally natural.

Nothing but a jar of oil

The widow of one of the sons of the prophets comes to Elisha with an alarming problem (II Kings 4:1):

> *"The creditor is coming to take my two children to be his slaves."*

The rest of the story reveals classic principles of the anointing (vv. 2-7):

> *So Elisha said to her, "What shall I do for you? Tell me, what do you have in the house?"*

The first principle here is that God is not asking for what we don't have, but for what we do have. This echoes the words that come out of the burning bush to Moses, who is complaining of his inadequacy (Exodus 4:2):

> *"What is that in your hand?" And he said, "A rod."*

The shepherd's rod is for Moses the symbol of his failed life: exiled from Pharaoh's court, he has spent forty years tending sheep in oblivion. For both Moses and the widow, the circumstances are discouraging. But in each case God has a plan. For Moses, the rod—the only thing in his hand—becomes the very means God uses to release a display of His power and liberate Israel from slavery. For the widow, the jar of oil—the only thing in her house—becomes the means of delivering her sons from slavery. There is no need to produce some great thing for God to bless; the humble things that we already have are what God uses.

Further, oil makes a clear picture of the anointing, which—to say it once again—literally means oil applied (v.2):

> *And she said, "Your maidservant has nothing in the house but a jar of oil."*

The principle to see here about the anointing is simply that a little is enough to begin with. Those who feel that only great men of God who address thousands and perform great miracles have a true anointing miss the message. Jesus describes this error when He tells the story of the servants to whom are entrusted various amounts of money (Matthew 25:14-30). The one who has received the least thinks that having so little, compared with those who have more, means that there is nothing significant for him to do. Jesus says the master of the servants rebukes the timidity of the one with little, and condemns him to destruction. The anointing is never to be underestimated; what appears to be insignificant is actually connected with eternity and has infinite potential. A little anointing is enough, because if we use it, it will increase, as the story of the widow goes on to reveal (II Kings 4:3-6):

Then he said, "Go, borrow vessels from everywhere, from all your neighbors—empty vessels; do not gather just a few. And when you have come in, you shall shut the door behind you and your sons; then pour it into all those vessels, and set aside the full ones." So she went from him and shut the door behind her and her sons, who brought the vessels to her; and she poured it out. Now it came to pass, when the vessels were full, that she said to her son, "Bring me another vessel." And he said to her, "There is not another vessel." So the oil ceased.

Active pursuit of ministry

There is another point here. Finding places to put the anointing may require a search. That is, just as the widow's sons ransack the town for more vessels, so we are to seek ways to use the anointing. There are people all around us whose empty hearts are in need of the touch of the Holy Spirit; there are situations worse than our own that we can change by sharing what we have of the power of God. Looking for places to pour the oil is what the anointing demands. The boys are not passive, but active in seeking empty vessels until no more can be found. As long as there is an empty vessel the oil flows, and not until the opportunities come to an end does the oil stop.

Lest some take what I am saying to mean that everyone should evangelize the neighborhood, I will point out that not all are evangelists, but only some (Ephesians 4:11):

And He gave some...evangelists.

There are many more ways of sharing the anointing besides evangelism: there is teaching and giving and showing mercy—to name a few. And we should be careful not to expect of ourselves, or of others, a ministry and gifting that we have not been given. But whatever our anointing—whatever our ministry and gifting, we are to be active in pursuing every outlet available to us.

Children and the anointing

Yet another thought here is that children can be effective in anointed ministry. The widow expects her sons to help in the important work she is about. She does not use them as a last resort, only after trying to enlist others more worthy or more experienced. She sees that the work is not complicated, but straightforward, and is not just for grownups. And she expects that her children will be as effective as anyone in helping to use the anointing. The boys themselves show no sign of reluctance, apparently giving themselves without hesitation to the task.

Children today—as in Elisha's time—are not only capable, but in some ways more perfectly suited to experiencing God's power than adults. In fact, Jesus points out that it is adults who must become as children, and not the other way around, if we are to experience the Kingdom at all (Matthew 18:3):

> *Assuredly I say to you, unless you...become as little children, you will by no means enter the kingdom of heaven.*

The legacy of the anointing

The last detail in this story gives us a beautiful picture of the way the anointing and grace flow together. Everything about God is part of everything else about Him, and the manifestation of His power and the free gift of grace go together. Not only is the anointing itself freely given, but the grace of God—His abundant giving in so many ways—is precisely what the anointing brings to us (II Kings 4:7):

> *Then she came and told the man of God. And he said, "Go, sell the oil and pay your debt; and you and your sons live on the rest."*

As the anointing invades our lives, grace is released to cancel past debts. Thank God for forgiving and forgetting the debts of the past. The damage done to us by ourselves and others, and the failures for which we suffer and feel shame are paid for by the grace of our Lord Jesus Christ. Here in this story is illustrated as well as anywhere the gracious effect of the anointing, as Jesus describes His ministry (Luke 4:18):

> *"To preach deliverance to the captives...to set at liberty those who are oppressed."*

The anointing by its very nature does much more than display outward power; it works inside hurting hearts to bring freedom and hope.

But when the issues of the past are resolved, the work of grace has only begun. Because besides paying our past debts, the anointing of the Holy Spirit becomes something to live on, empowering our lives with a legacy of blessing. When we have been touched by miraculous grace we are never the same again because we see ourselves and others—and God!—in a new way. Life takes on a depth and a joy that reflect an encounter with the infinite Spirit of God. And the more of the Holy Spirit's anointing we experience, the deeper the flow of grace, and the greater the sense of connection with an infinite God.

All of this is to say that the gracious flow of the Holy Spirit that is the anointing is so much more than forgiveness for the past. It is the breath that we were meant to breathe, the fuel that we were meant to consume, the story that we were meant to tell, and the music we were meant to play. When the anointing cancels our debts we have relief almost beyond words; but when the anointing continues to flow with life we have purpose, fulfillment, vision, relationship, significance—all the things the heart longs for.

Grace forgives, but grace also gives, and the giving never ends. It is the nature of this gracious anointing to flow infinitely—like an endowment that just keeps producing interest—because its source is the heart of an infinite God. Our debts are paid, and we can live abundantly on all the rest that continues to flow.

4

THE SHUNAMMITE

Getting close to the anointing

The next story in the life of Elisha reveals the hungry heart of a woman with a need greater than at first appears (II Kings 4: 8):

> *Now it happened one day that Elisha went to Shunem, where there was a notable woman, and she constrained him to eat some food. So it was, as often as he passed by, he turned in there to eat some food.*

On the surface this woman stands in contrast to the widow in the previous story. This woman is "notable," meaning that she is a person of influence and—as it turns out—some wealth. At first we may see her invitation for the prophet to come to dinner as simple hospitality. But the hospitality becomes a regular practice, and with each visit the woman sees something in Elisha that stirs her spirit, so that in time a larger motive emerges (v. 9, 10):

> *And she said to her husband, "Look now, I know that this is a holy man of God, who passes by us regularly. Please, let us make a small upper room on the wall; and let us put a bed for him there, and a table and a chair and a lampstand; so it will be, whenever he comes to us, he can turn in there."*

She recognizes the holiness of Elisha and she wants to get even closer to the man of God because in fact she wants to get closer to God. So her heart contrives a way to have Elisha stay longer, and with her husband's agreement, the prophet's chamber is built.

This is an important principle: People who love the anointing want to be around anointed people. The anointing can be cultivated in several ways, including, as we have seen, through music and worship. But because the anointing is transferable from

LICENSE

person to person, it is always useful when those who are hungry and thirsty for more of God can be with those who carry with them a heightened sense of the presence of God.

The price to pay

There is, however, a price to pay for being exposed to the anointing; the price is that the anointing exposes us. As the story of the Shunammite unfolds, Elisha one day visits the prophet's chamber and sends his servant Gehazi to summon the lady of the house. When she comes, Elisha thanks her for her faithful kindness and asks how he can repay her (v. 13):

> *"What can I do for you? Do you want me to speak on your behalf to the king or to the commander of the army?"*

Her answer is what we might expect of someone already well established (v. 13):

> *And she answered, "I dwell among my own people."*

She is saying, in other words, No thanks—I'm fine; I have no needs; I am satisfied with my life. But Elisha senses that there really is a need, and presses Gehazi for further information. Eventually, Gehazi reports (v.14),

> *"Actually, she has no son, and her husband is old."*

And this, it becomes clear, is the story of her life; the secret of her heart is laid open. Here is a woman who has everything materially and socially—"a notable woman." But she has never had the son that her heart longs for, and the heir that her culture requires of a wife. Think of her as year after year passes and she remains childless. When she is first married, there are knowing smiles from the other young women carrying their infants with them to the market. As the dreaded months and then years go by, she tries not to gaze too wistfully as the neighborhood toddlers romp into adolescence, but she can't help noticing whispered conversations that end abruptly as she approaches. And she sees her husband's sadness when he watches the other men working with their strapping sons. Years turn into decades and her concern turns to grief as her body begins to age. Besides, as Gehazi points out, her husband is old, a fact which suggests declining virility. Hope of conception dwindles.

Fulfilling her role as a prominent woman about town, the Shunammite buries her heartache in a round of social engagements and charitable projects. She perfects the air of prosperous serenity as maturity settles upon her with matronly grace.

But then this man of God comes to town, and there is something at once fascinating and disturbing about him. She feels a longing stirring in her spirit when he comes into her home; it is like the longing for a child; but, then again, it is a different kind of longing—a longing for God that is much deeper—and a strange hope dawns in her heart. Then one day Gehazi tells her that the man of God would like to see her again, and Elisha says (II Kings 4:16),

> *"About this time next year you shall embrace a son."*

The disappointment of so many years—so many months—is a pain only just below the surface. She recoils from its sting with a flash of denial (v. 16)—

> *And she said, "No, my lord. Man of God, do not lie to your maidservant!"*

She simply has no emotional reserve, no more tolerance for disappointment. But the anointing has touched her life and there is no turning back. The strange hope—a hope beyond all reason—rises uncontrollably (v. 17),

> *And the woman conceived, and bore a son when the appointed time had come, of which Elisha had told her.*

Regretting the anointing

Events for the Shunammite have begun to seem too good to be true. Once childless and grieving, she becomes fulfilled and happy as the mother of a baby boy. As he grows, she experiences all the pride and delight that has been only in her imagination before. Now she cannot imagine a time when his presence did not brighten the house with his chatter and kisses, his playthings underfoot, his bedtimes and bath times. All too soon he leaves her side for adventures outdoors, playing with neighbor children.

Then one day, the boy asks if he can visit his father overseeing the reapers in the field. Well, why not? she likely thinks. He is now quite a big boy and able to walk a distance by himself, and besides, the workers are actually just within sight, and God will take care of him. Everything will be all right. So the boy (II Kings 4:18-20)

> went out to his father, to the reapers. And he said to his father, "My head, my head!" So he said to a servant, "Carry him to his mother." When he had taken him and brought him to his mother, he sat on her knees till noon, and then died.

To become involved with the anointing is to place ourselves at risk, because the anointing flows in the spiritual realm by a different set of values than the natural realm. Paul says that spiritually (II Corinthians 4:18),

> We do not look at the things which are seen, but at the things which are not seen. For the things which are seen are temporary, but the things which are not seen are eternal.

And (II Corinthians 5:7),

> We walk by faith, not by sight.

We can assume, then, that the visible natural realm—which is what we most easily see and experience—will be more or less out of step with the invisible spiritual realm. What is important and reasonable in one realm is likely unimportant and unreasonable in the other.

At any rate, the Shunammite woman's walk by faith is surely challenged when it appears that disaster has befallen her dream-come-true. What had been a wonderful blessing suddenly is turned to an even greater disappointment than all the disappointments that had gone before. To have touched the anointing at all now seems a liability.

Two things, however, are clear from what follows. One is that this mother knows that if anything can be done to help her son, it will be by the anointing (II Kings 4:21,22):

> *And she went up and laid [her dead son] on the bed of the man of God, shut the door upon him, and went out. Then she called to her husband, and said, "Please send me one of the young men and one of the donkeys, that I may run to the man of God and come back."*

The other is that, against all visible and reasonable evidence, she has hope. When her husband questions her travel plans she says (v.23),

> *"It is well."*

As she approaches Elisha, his servant asks on behalf of the prophet (v.26),

> *"Is it well with you? Is it well with your husband? Is it well with the child?" And she answered, "It is well."*

But then she stoops and holds onto Elisha's feet and accuses (v. 28),

> *"Did I ask for a son from my lord? Did I not say, 'Do not deceive me'?"*

We see here a dilemma of faith and frustration: the woman is saying on the one hand that everything is fine (meaning, "I know God is in control of these things."). But on the other hand she is complaining that God might better have left her alone in the first place (meaning, "I don't like the way He is controlling things.").

One of the most important principles of the anointing is this: if we want to experience the presence and power of God, we must learn to trust Him to get it right, without putting expectations or limits on what He does. If we are always anxious about whether we will receive—or have taken from us—some desirable outcome, it may be that we are looking at what is visible but temporary in the natural realm, rather than at what is invisible but eternal in the spiritual realm.

The anointing always challenges our perception of things, and there may be times when we—like the Shunammite—also complain that perhaps we would be better off not to be involved in this supernatural business for which our natural mind is not at all suited. Seen from a natural point of view, we would indeed be better off without the anointing—given the uncertainties. But as we move along, the anointing teaches us to accept the will of Him who is the source of the power. We find ourselves in collaboration with the Spirit, learning, as Marc Dupont says, that "God is the Great I Am, and I am the great I'm not." This is actually one of the loveliest benefits of the anointing—the relief that this resignation brings. To seek the anointing unconditionally is to relax in the will of God, and to be so content in the Father's goodness that we let go of our own need to control.

Transferring the anointing

Elisha quickly sees the problem—that the woman's son has died—and he takes immediate action (II Kings 4:29):

> *Then he said to Gehazi, "Get yourself ready, and take my staff in your hand, and be on your way. If you meet anyone, do not greet him; and if anyone greets you, do not answer him; but lay my staff on the face of the child."*

The prophet puts into practice a feature of the anointing—that it is transferable. The anointing from one person or place can be transferred to another, sometimes at a distance and sometimes through objects. The point of Gehazi laying the staff of Elisha on the face of the dead child is that, even without Elisha being physically present, the power of God upon him might be released through something he has touched. This seems bizarre until we recall that something similar happens through Paul in New Testament times (Acts 19:11,12):

> *Now God worked unusual miracles by the hands of Paul, so that even handkerchiefs or aprons were brought from his body to the sick, and the diseases left them and the evil spirits went out of them.*

While we certainly should be careful not to assume that this is to be a common occurrence (these are "unusual miracles"), the interesting possibility exists that God's power—or the anointing—

can at times be transferred in surprising ways.

Multiple applications of the anointing

As it happens, this attempt to transfer the anointing by sending Gehazi to the boy with Elisha's staff proves ineffective, after all (II Kings 4:31):

> *Now Gehazi went on ahead of them, and laid the staff on the*
> *face of the child; but there was neither voice nor hearing.*
> *Therefore he went back to meet him, and told him, saying,*
> *"The child has not awakened."*

Sometimes, for no reason we can tell, the anointing does not flow as we expect. This does not mean that, since the first attempt to release the anointing does not work, we should give up; rather we should understand that the situation calls for further measures.

So Elisha himself goes to the deathbed, and, shutting the door, he first prays; then (v.34)

> *He went up and lay on the child, and put his mouth on his*
> *mouth, his eyes on his eyes, and his hands on his hands; and*
> *he stretched himself out on the child.*

Since his staff applied by Gehazi produces no satisfactory result, Elisha applies his own body to the corpse. We might doubt the wisdom of the attempted use of the staff in the first place, but we could also ask why this intimate—and morbid—touching of the corpse be attempted next. Why isn't the prayer enough? One answer is simply to point out that Jesus sometimes speaks a command, as with Simon's mother-in-law (Luke 4:39):

> *So He stood over her and rebuked the fever, and it left her.*
> *And immediately she arose,*

but other times He lays His hands on people (Luke 4:40):

> *And He laid His hands on every one of them and healed*
> *them.*

And still other times He uses saliva (John 9:6,7):

> *He spat on the ground and made clay with the saliva; and He anointed the eyes of the blind man with the clay. And He said to him, "Go, wash...." So he...washed, and came back seeing;*

and (Mark 7:33),

> *He...put His fingers in his ears, and He spat and touched his tongue.*

Moving in the anointing is not the same as following a set of how-to directions or rules, because the power of the Holy Spirit cannot be conveniently packaged for the consumer. I am describing in this book what I call "lessons in the anointing," by which I mean that there are things to understand about how the anointing works, without suggesting that there are ways to control the anointing. Nor do we crack the code, so to speak, by figuring out what words to say or actions to perform, because sometimes the Holy Spirit does what we expect, and sometimes not. People who are learning how to move in the anointing are basically learning to submit to—rather than control— the Holy Spirit.

But, further, we see that even when Elisha performs the prophetic act of lying on the child's body, the miracle is incomplete. This is already the second application of the anointing (the first is Elisha's staff laid on the body by Gehazi). And if we expect that now there will be a successful resurrection, we are disappointed. But at least something supernatural is going on (II Kings 4:34):

> *The flesh of the child became warm.*

If we think that our attempts at moving in the anointing have failed because we don't have instant and complete results, we set for ourselves a higher standard than the Bible! Even Jesus performs at least one miracle in stages (Mark 8:23-25):

> *So He took the blind man by the hand and led him out of the town. And when He had spit on his eyes and put His hands on him, He asked him if he saw anything. And he looked up and said, "I see men like trees, walking." Then He put His hands on his eyes again and made him look up. And he was restored and saw everyone clearly.*

Following precedent

A common mistake among believers may be misapplying the Scriptures by assuming that the way the anointing has been released once will be the way it always is released. But—as we have already seen—Jesus uses a variety of methods when He heals people in the Gospels. And if we were to note all the miracles in the Bible, we would see that God has always worked a variety of manifestations of His power by a variety of means.

On the other hand, sometimes a method is repeated. The story of the Shunammite's son being brought to life closely resembles a miracle in the career of Elisha's mentor Elijah (I Kings 17:21,22):

> *And he stretched himself out on the child three times, and cried out to the LORD and said, "O LORD my God, I pray, let this child's soul come back to him."...and the soul of the child came back to him, and he revived.*

How does Elisha know that this is one of those times to follow precedent? Perhaps the Holy Spirit tells him by a clear impression in those moments of prayer before he lies on the child. Or perhaps as he seeks the direction of the Spirit he remembers Elijah's miracle and figures this is at least worth a try.

Again, what is important to understand is that the anointing is dynamic rather than static. To experience the anointing successfully requires sensitivity to the Spirit, as moving and alive. Jesus describes this dynamic as the wind (John 3:8):

> *The wind blows where it wishes, and you hear the sound of it, but cannot tell where it comes from and where it goes. So is everyone who is born of the Spirit.*

As the wind blows, so the Holy Spirit moves—and so His people move with Him. Paul points out that (Romans 8:14)

> *As many as are led by the Spirit of God, these are sons of God.*

Characteristic of God's people is their affinity to the leading of the Holy Spirit. This means that neither Bible chapter and verse, nor the examples of godly people, are enough to go by. We need the revelation of the Holy Spirit if we are going to find our way in the spiritual realm. The Holy Spirit will use the Bible, and He will use the influence of others. But ultimately the leading must be His. As Jesus says of the good Shepherd (John 10:4),

>*The sheep follow him, for they know his voice.*

As Elisha continues to seek the leading of the Holy Spirit (I Kings 4:35),

>*He returned and walked back and forth in the house,*

praying with some desperation, no doubt, and he feels led once again to lie on the body. He has already tried that, and it has only been partly successful. But it is worth applying the anointing repeatedly if there is any hope of a full resurrection. At last the power of God is fully released and (v. 35)

>*the child sneezed seven times, and…opened his eyes.*

When the woman receives her son back to life, she experiences for a second time the flow of anointing that miraculously alters her life, relieving her grief and putting her in touch with the God of Israel.

5

THE SONS OF THE PROPHETS

Death in the pot

Among the amazing things about the Kingdom of God is that God takes the risk of sharing ministry with imperfect people. He has a reason for this: Paul says (II Corinthians 4:7),

> *We have this treasure in earthen vessels, that the excellence of the power may be of God and not of us.*

In other words, our imperfection in ministry only enhances it. If we were perfect, the ministry might appear to be from us. The problem thus created, however, is obvious: our involvement introduces the possibility of corruption. The fact that God takes this risk is useful to remember when we consider sharing ministry with others. Imperfect like us, others bring to ministry the potential for doing more harm than good. This is exactly what Elisha faces in the next story, and it is well for us to see how he handles the disaster of an attempted ministry gone awry.

Meeting with the sons of the prophets—evidently a group in ministry training—Elisha announces (II Kings 4:38),

> *"Put on the large pot, and boil stew for the sons of the prophets."*

By definition a stew is a collection of many things brought together in a mixture, a fairly simple picture of spiritual ministry in a group of people. Unlike separate dishes from which we can take what suits us, stew offers a conglomeration of flavors, textures, and nutrients all intermingled and influencing each other. One bad ingredient and the stew is ruined, and everyone eating it is affected (v.39):

> *So one went out into the field to gather herbs, and found a wild*

*vine, and gathered from it a lap full of wild gourds, and came
and sliced them into the pot of stew, though they did not know
what they were.*

If this is a spiritual picture, then we see the possibility of one
person unwisely adding to the general mix of ministry something
that might be dangerous. Doesn't the man of God know the
danger of allowing an inexperienced person to contribute to what is
being offered to all? Shouldn't he be more careful by feeding the
people only what he himself brings for their consumption?

In fact, the stew is disastrous (v.40):

*Then they served it to the men to eat. Now it happened, as
they were eating the stew, that they cried out and said, "O man
of God, there is death in the pot!" And they could not eat it.*

One ingredient, unwisely added by an inept contributor, brings
poison and death. A natural reaction to this story, as a metaphor of
ministry, would be to resolve to keep even closer control over who
is allowed to minister. But as the story continues and we see the
anointing at work, we find another solution. Although damage has
been done and many people have been poisoned, Elisha calmly
brings healing to the situation (v. 41):

*So he said, "Then bring some flour." And he put it into the
pot, and said, "Serve it to the people, that they may eat."
And there was nothing harmful in the pot.*

I understand the flour to represent the anointing. Jesus is the
Bread of Life, and what He touches is healed and restored. When
Paul teaches the Corinthians about the oversight of ministry in
church meetings, he doesn't say that prophetic messages ought to
be disallowed because of the danger of error. Instead, he explains
that prophecies are to be allowed on condition that they are subject
to discernment (I Corinthians 14:29):

Let two or three prophets speak, and let the others judge.

The point is that if wrong things added to the mix of
ministry do harm, the harm can be undone. We are not to fear the
stew of variety in ministry, as though the Holy Spirit is not able to

help us to sort out truth from error. His presence and His wisdom can bless the good and detoxify the bad.

I once experienced the Holy Spirit's protection in a remarkable way. I had traveled to a meeting with a small group of people for whom I felt responsible. Much that went on in the meeting was true and good. But one speaker was introduced who began to develop what I sensed was a false ministry. I was concerned for the people with me, and I began to pray that the Lord would prevent this message from causing them any harm. Imagine my surprise and amazement afterward when I attempted to discuss with my group what the speaker had said, and each of the five or six people confessed that they had fallen asleep during that part of the meeting—and had no idea what had gone on! The anointing removes the death in the pot.

I am not suggesting by this that we should put ourselves in harm's way by deliberately receiving what we know to be false ministry. But we need to be open to unproven situations, rather than rejecting the stew of ministry out of fear.

A practice among some charismatics may, by this standard, be less than scriptural. Sometimes in meetings where it is expected that members of the congregation may offer prophetic messages, prophecies are pre-judged. It is announced that anyone who has a word they feel is from the Holy Spirit should approach a designated person who is authorized to allow the word to be spoken to the meeting if it is thought to be valid. This prophetic "filter" is to spare the congregation the danger of false prophecy. But should the congregation be spared? Or should messages, rather, be judged by everyone present—confirmed or rejected by leaders, perhaps, but out in the open nevertheless? (An exception might be limits set on someone whose past attempts at prophetic ministry have been seriously out of order—as clearly unscriptural, spoken in bitterness or pride, or in other ways unacceptable.)

The way of the Spirit is variety (I Corinthians 12:4-6):

> *Now there are diversities of gifts, but the same Spirit. There are differences of ministries, but the same Lord. And there are*

diversities of activities, but it is the same God who works all in all.

One of the marks of spiritual maturity is that we celebrate the differences in the Body of Christ. And if there are differences, there are also risks. First, if we depart in any way from the established and accepted doctrines and practices of our group and its leaders, there is the risk that we may encounter error in others. Second is the risk that others may encounter error in us. Think of the man who adds wild gourds to the pot of stew for the sons of the prophets. If Elisha's reaction had been different—if he had, instead, recoiled with fear or if he had flared out with orthodox indignation—what would have been the result in the man at fault? He may well have resolved, at best, never to offer anything again, or, at worst, to leave the group so as not to be shamed. And what of the others? They, too, might have been so intimidated that they would never risk being in error, and therefore never pursue the truth in a way that takes them beyond rigid definitions.

Rather, Elisha models for us the calm assurance of a man whose God is big enough to protect His people. He simply applies the anointing (represented in the flour) and the stew is made harmless, nourishing hungry people.

More than enough

The next story is reminiscent of Jesus multiplying a small lunch to feed thousands. The proportions are different, but the results are similar (II Kings 4:42-44):

> *Then a man came from Baal-shalisha, and brought the man of God bread of the firstfruits, twenty loaves of barley bread, and newly ripened grain in his knapsack. And he said, "Give it to the people, that they may eat." And his servant said, "What? Shall I set this before one hundred men?" He said again "Give it to the people, that they may eat; for thus says the LORD: 'They shall eat and have some left over.'" So he set it before them; and they ate and had some left over.*

When the anointing—the power of God—touches a

situation, it is not a matter of wondering if the power is sufficient, but of expecting an overflow. In addition to the multiplying of food to feed thousands, Jesus also blesses the disciples, who had fished all night and caught nothing, with the promise of a miraculous catch (John 21:6):

> *And He said to them, "Cast the net on the right side of the boat, and you will find some." So they cast, and now they were not able to draw it in because of the multitude of fish.*

The familiar and inspiring Twenty-third Psalm includes David's four-word testimony of receiving more than enough (v. 5):

> *My cup runs over.*

Amos prophesies to future generations God's promise of His goodness (Amos 9:13):

> *"Behold, the days are coming," says the LORD, "when the plowman shall overtake the reaper, and the treader of grapes him who sows seed; the mountains shall drip with sweet wine."*

These phrases are all about extravagance of blessing. For the plowman to overtake the reaper means that in autumn the harvest is so abundant that the reapers are still coping with the quantity when spring arrives and it is time to plant again.

A characteristic of the power of God is that it provides exceeding abundance—more than enough. When we are used to ordinary procedures and results, learning to expect God's extravagance in our life through the anointing takes some adjustment.

One of the great success stories of evangelism is of Dwight L. Moody, whose personal testimony reflects the abundance that follows the anointing. Richard Ellsworth Day, in *Bush Aglow: The life story of Dwight Lyman Moody, commoner of Northfield*, reports the explanation for the watershed change in his ministry:

> The fruits of his preaching had been small and few. In distress he walked the streets of [New York] by night—'Oh God, anoint me with Thy Spirit!'…. God heard him…and gave him right on the street what he had begged for…. Words could not express the Influence upon him…. He had been trying to pump water out of a well that seemed dry…. He pumped with all his might and little water came…. Then God had made his soul like an Artesian well that could never fail of water.

Overnight Moody experienced a transformation from struggling efforts and meager results to an evangelistic career leading perhaps hundreds of thousands to Christ in America and Great Britain in the mid-nineteenth century—an abundance beyond what anyone could have asked or thought.

6

NAAMAN

Compelled by need to seek the anointing

Clearly, one of the paths to the anointing is the way of loss and brokenness. As with Moody, whose personal spiritual dryness and ineffectiveness in ministry compelled him to seek the power of the Holy Spirit, the experience of Naaman in II Kings 5 is a story of desperation. On the surface, Naaman is a successful man with the world at his feet, as it were (v. 1):

> *Now Naaman, commander of the army of the king of Syria, was a great and honorable man in the eyes of his master, because by him the LORD had given victory to Syria. He was also a mighty man of valor.*

There is nothing here to indicate that Naaman understands his military success to be by God's favor. To all appearance, his achievements are hard-won and highly rewarded, and he can congratulate himself on having arrived. Naaman is not the sort of man we would expect to be looking for help from anyone—least of all from a prophet of Israel.

But for all the outward fulfillment, Naaman is a desperate man, because, as the end of this verse reveals,

> *He was a leper.*

Lepers not only were condemned to a slow physical deterioration, sometimes to death, but they became social outcasts, as well. Of what value are memories of military triumph and honor at the king's court now that leprosy has risen as a specter of ruin?

In this place of brokenness, the great Naaman finds himself doing what he could not otherwise have imagined doing: he listens to the advice of a little Hebrew girl, his wife's servant (II Kings 5:3):

> *Then she said to her mistress, "If only my master were with the prophet who is in Samaria! For he would heal him of his leprosy."*

With the Syrian king's approval and letter of introduction, Naaman goes to Samaria, the capital city of Israel, in quest of the anointing—the power of God—to heal him.

The uselessness of status

The story begins to take on a sadly comical twist, however, when we see the broken Naaman departing his home, propped up by the symbols of his wealth and status (II Kings 5:5):

> *So he departed and took with him ten talents of silver, six thousand shekels of gold, and ten changes of clothing.*

It would seem that Naaman—now but a shell of the great man he once was—is not broken quite enough. He pursues the anointing—the power of God—with the trappings of human power. He has the right goal, but completely mistakes the means, as the story continues to show.

Misunderstanding the anointing

The Syrian captain goes to find the man of God (II Kings 5:9):

> *Then Naaman went with his horses and chariot, and he stood at the door of the house of Elisha.*

What happens next illustrates the false expectations that people can have of how the anointing works. Naaman arrives surrounded by his impressive material things—a mistake in itself. But when Elisha sends a messenger to tell the Syrian to wash seven times in the Jordan, Naaman's response betrays his mistaken assumptions (II Kings 5:11,12):

> *But Naaman became furious, and went away and said, "Indeed, I said to myself, 'He will surely come out to me, and stand and call on the name of the LORD his God, and wave*

his hand over the place, and heal the leprosy.'" ...So he
turned and went away in a rage.

For us to assume we know how the anointing will be administered, and how the power will manifest, can lead to confusion at best; at worst, it can lead to a rejection of the real thing. Naaman is angry and goes away, because what he thinks the anointing will be like is not the way it actually is. A logical scenario plays out in his mind in which the prophet will come out to him and strike an authoritative pose and intone a spiritual prayer. Naaman's expectation is that this is what prophets are supposed to do. But when it doesn't happen—when his expectations are violated—he is so offended that he almost misses his encounter with the power of God.

The gospel story of the Christ Who comes to earth for our redemption has this perverse feature, that (John 1:11)

He came to His own, and His own did not receive Him.

The reason they do not receive Him is because of their mistaken assumptions. They assume their Messiah will be a military hero who will rout the Roman occupation and reestablish the kingdom of David. When He comes it is in simplicity and meekness and to proclaim the Kingdom of God in a way never thought of by the religiously opinionated. And religious people have been rejecting the true Anointed One ever since, because He does not fit their expectations.

The danger is that people who profess to seek after God may miss Him because of preconceived ideas, doctrinal systems or traditional paradigms. An irony among conservative believers is that on the one hand we require that every spiritual experience must be defined in the Bible. If there isn't an example of it in the Bible, then we cannot accept it, even though the record shows that God rarely does things the same way twice. And on the other hand, we reason, experiences similar to those that happened to people in the Bible could not possibly happen to us—simply because they are supernatural.

Among more charismatic or Pentecostal believers there may

be an equal danger in the other extreme. Assuming that because someone else has had a spiritual experience—in the Bible or in church history—that happened in a certain way, or that produced a certain result, the expectation is that others will have a similar experience.

Naaman's "I said to myself…" is the very thing that almost costs him his healing, just as our unfounded notions of how God does what He does may cost us the anointing. It is not faith when we decide ahead of time the sorts of ways God is allowed to work. Nor is it faith when, inspired by a story, we try to duplicate an experience. It is faith when, seeking God in humility, we open ourselves up to the Holy Spirit's elegant creativity in meeting our hearts in His own way.

Letting go in order to receive

Why are Elisha's instructions to Naaman so offensive (II Kings 5:10)?—

> *"Go and wash in the Jordan seven times."*

Is it just that Naaman expects something grander? Or is it the Jordan itself? (v. 12)

> *"Are not the Abanah and the Pharpar, the rivers of*
> *Damascus, better than all the waters of Israel? Could I not*
> *wash in them and be clean?"*

Perhaps it is the combination of both that represents to Naaman a letting go of everything that is his identity. His national pride in his homeland is offended, as is his sense of self-importance. But if he wants his healing, he must let it all go. He must strip himself of his symbols of dignity and power and descend naked into these inferior waters.

There, skinny-dipping in the Jordan River, the great Naaman becomes an ordinary man—we might almost say a somewhat ridiculous ordinary man, making a spectacle of himself, on the outside chance that this anointing will actually work. None of the visible things make sense—the public bathing, doing it seven times, and in this, of all rivers! But inwardly his heart is being prepared for an encounter with God by losing all pretensions to respectability and logical method.

God's ways tend not to make sense to our natural mind, as He says in Isaiah 55:8,9,

> "For My thoughts are not your thoughts, neither are your ways My ways," says the LORD. "For as the heavens are higher than the earth, so are My ways higher than your ways, and My thoughts than your thoughts."

Job, after all the arguments and discussion concerning the role of God in the events of his life, finally admits that his human opinions about God mean nothing (Job 42:3-6):

> "I have uttered what I did not understand, things too wonderful for me, which I did not know.... You said, 'I will question you, and you shall answer me'.... I have heard of You by the hearing of the ear, But now my eye sees You. Therefore I abhor myself, And repent in dust and ashes."

When Job begins to see things—the things of God and the things of man—as they really are, he is embarrassed by what he had thought was wisdom.

When the seventy return to Jesus, full of excitement over the anointing they have seen released in ministry, Jesus (Luke 10:21)

> rejoiced in the Spirit, and said, "I praise You, Father, Lord of heaven and earth, that You have hidden these things from the wise and prudent and revealed them to babes."

Paul, writing to the Corinthians, quotes Isaiah 29:14 (I Corinthians 1:19):

> For it is written, "I will destroy the wisdom of the wise, and bring to nothing the understanding of the prudent."

And the apostle goes on to ask (v. 20),

> Where is the wise? Where is the scribe? Where is the disputer of this age? Has not God made foolish the wisdom of this world?

Then he offers this comfort—or challenge, depending on our point of view (v. 27,28):

> *But God has chosen the foolish things of the world to put to shame the wise, and God has chosen the weak things of the world to put to shame the things which are mighty, and the base things of the world and the things which are despised, God has chosen.*

It would seem that God likes foolishness—not the folly of self-trust or negligence, but the foolishness of the simple-hearted who trust Him irrationally. Paul also tells the Corinthians (I Corinthians 3:18),

> *Let no one deceive himself. If anyone among you seems to be wise in this age, let him become a fool that he may become wise.*

Becoming as a child

As though he had not been reduced enough, Naaman has one more humbling stage to experience. As he completes the required seven dips in the Jordan, he is healed by the anointing released through the word of Elisha (II Kings 5:14):

> *His flesh was restored.*

Yes!

Whole again!

It has been worth the trip!

The desperation that leads the Syrian captain past his pride and preconceptions to seek the touch of God is fulfilled in this wonderful moment of healing. Perhaps Naaman's mind begins to race with thoughts of his triumphant journey home, the life he can return to with his wife, and at the king's court, and joining his warriors once more in battle and conquest.

But he finds—and it is too late for second thoughts!—that the anointing comes at a price. With the restoration of his flesh from the leprosy, there comes a radical change (II Kings 5:14):

And his flesh was restored like the flesh of a little child.

The sun-bronzed warrior—the hairy-chested, callused-handed man's man—is transformed: his skin now has the soft smoothness of a baby. Perhaps even the leprosy is something he can, in the early stages, disguise. A telltale spot here and there might be hidden by clothing. But this is a total makeover: his old tough macho self is gone, and in its place a new vulnerable childlike identity becomes evident to all that meet him.

Jesus teaches His disciples that the only valid approach to the Kingdom of God is in childlikeness (Matthew 18:2-4):

> *And Jesus called a little child to Him, and set him in the midst of them, and said, "Assuredly I say to you, unless you are converted and become as little children, you will by no means enter the kingdom of heaven."*

The anointing does more than heal our bodies and empower us for service. We are changed by a meekness and a simplicity that always characterizes those who have encountered God in a deep way.

It might seem that those who have been privileged to have a powerful spiritual experience could tend rather to be boastful of what they have seen and heard. But Moses, having met God amid the lightening and thunder, fire and smoke of Sinai, is described as (Numbers 12:3)

> *very humble, more than all men who were on the face of the earth.*

And Isaiah, who (Isaiah 6:1)

> *saw the Lord sitting on a throne, high and lifted up, and the train of His robe filled the temple,*

responds (v.5),

> *"Woe is me, for I am undone! Because I am a man of unclean lips, and I dwell in the midst of a people of unclean lips; For my eyes have seen the King, The LORD of hosts."*

Those who seek an encounter with God had best prepare to be changed and simplified and humbled. There is no room for maintaining our dignity if we want to be invaded by the Spirit of Him who (Philippians 2:7)

> *made Himself of no reputation, taking the form of a servant.*

Spirit versus letter

There are several more things to learn from Naaman. These follow his encounter with the power of God, when his perspective has been altered so that he is seeing from a spiritual, rather than from a natural, point of view (II Kings 5:15):

> *Then he returned to the man of God, he and all his aides, and came and stood before him; and he said, "Indeed, now I know that there is no God in all the earth, except in Israel."*

It might be safe to say that any encounter with the anointing changes our perspective, because we see things more as they really are. Naaman, because he has been touched by God's power, understands now that the God of Israel is the only true God. And it is in this knowledge that he asks Elisha (who this time consents to meet with him) for his approval on two related matters. Elisha's reply is, I think, significant.

The first matter of concern for Naaman is that he, a Gentile, wants to worship the Lord God of Israel (II Kings 5:17):

> *"Please let your servant be given two mule-loads of earth; for your servant will no longer offer either burnt offering or sacrifice to other gods, but to the* LORD.*"*

It would seem that he is proposing to make some kind of altar with soil from the place where he has encountered the power of God. And, on this makeshift altar, he wants to offer sacrifices to the true God. We can hardly blame Naaman for wanting to take home something to keep him close to the anointing that has let him experience such healing, cleansing power. But sacrifices on an earthen altar? Sacrifices are for priests and prophets and kings of Israel to make on proper stone or bronze altars.

The second concern is Naaman's plan to make regular visits to a pagan temple. He explains that it will be his duty (II Kings 5:18):

"Yet in this thing may the LORD pardon your servant: when my master goes into the temple of Rimmon to worship there, and he leans on my hand, and I bow down in the temple of Rimmon—when I bow down in the temple of Rimmon, may the LORD please pardon your servant in this thing."

How do we reconcile Naaman's notions with a scriptural point of view? For this Gentile to offer sacrifices to the Lord on an altar built of souvenir earth from Israel transported to a heathen land has no support from the Levitical system of worship. And to go with his king to bow in a pagan temple would seem compromising at best. Yet Elisha gives his blessing to both (II Kings 5:19):

Then he said to him, "Go in peace."

Naaman experiences grace, and when we experience grace, the rules change. By this I mean that grace and Law are two different value systems. This is an Old Testament story, and it takes place long before the gospel of Jesus Christ replaces the Law, but there is a principle to be seen in Elisha's gracious words to Naaman from which we can learn.

Paul explains (I Timothy 1:8,9),

But we know that the law is good if one uses it lawfully, knowing this: that the law is not made for a righteous person, but for the lawless and insubordinate, for the ungodly and for sinners.

Rather than lay down the law to Naaman, Elisha recognizes in him a righteous intent, and allows for strictness to be set aside. And he agrees that although what he asks is not lawful, it is righteous.

Jesus tries to explain this to the religious legalists of His day when He talks about the Sabbath. They challenge Jesus' disciples picking grain to eat as they walk on the Sabbath, saying that it is unlawful to do, because technically they are performing the work of harvesting, and work is forbidden on the Sabbath. Jesus replies with the illustration that David and his men eat the consecrated showbread—unlawful for any but priests to eat—in order to serve a higher purpose. So it is, Jesus points out, with observing the

Sabbath; there is grace to use the Sabbath in helpful ways not technically permitted by the law (Mark 2:27,28):

> *And he said to them, "The Sabbath was made for man, and not man for the Sabbath. Therefore, the Son of Man is also Lord of the Sabbath."*

Paul, in explaining the difference between the Law and grace, says (II Corinthians 3:6),

> *the letter [the literal written law] kills, but the Spirit [the anointing] gives life.*

And he explains further that even the Old Covenant of the Jews was more about an inward encounter with God than racial identity and an outward physical sign (Romans 2:28,29):

> *For he is not a Jew who is one outwardly, nor is that circumcision which is outward in the flesh; but he is a Jew who is one inwardly, and circumcision is that of the heart, in the Spirit, and not in the letter.*

What Elisha perceives in Naaman is a right heart, because the anointing has brought him grace, and Elisha's, *"Go in peace,"* anticipates Paul's (Titus 1:15),

> *To the pure all things are pure.*

Jesus says (Matthew 5:8),

> *"Blessed are the pure in heart, for they shall see God."*

Which is first—the purity of heart or the encounter with God? Perhaps they go together. How do we become pure? Is it not by an encounter with a gracious God? And how do we encounter God? Is it not with a pure heart? Naaman resists at first, and almost misses both his cleansing and his encounter. But because he is willing at last to be reduced in obedience from self-importance to childlike simplicity, God changes everything for him. The anointing is released into Naaman because in his spirit he is receptive to grace—not because he fulfills religious ritual.

Speaking to people following outward religious rules, Jesus says that they and their kind always miss the inward reality. And he cites Naaman as an example of a man who has a right heart, and who gets what others miss (Luke 4:27):

"And many lepers were in Israel in the time of Elisha the prophet, and none of them was cleansed except Naaman the Syrian."

Naaman, a pagan whose heart is transformed by the anointing, comes closer to the truth and closer to God than many people in Israel. He breaks the rules, but he has favor with God, because God is not looking for rule-keepers so much as He is looking for God-seekers. Naaman passes the test—and he goes in peace.

Money and the anointing

Before we leave the story of Naaman, we need to notice how money relates to the anointing. There is an implication that when Naaman first goes to Elisha, seeking a healing for leprosy, the significant amount of wealth he carries is for a gift to the prophet. Elisha, by refusing to see Naaman at first, allows no opportunity for gift giving. There are likely several reasons for this.

First, if the anointing is a product of grace, then it is not Elisha's possession anyway. And he wants to impress Naaman with the fact that he is dealing with the eternal God, and not with a mere man.

Second, Naaman needs to have his self-sufficiency challenged. None of his greatness or power means anything to God. His wealth is irrelevant to the process of receiving the anointing. God's power is not given to the naturally powerful, as is written by another prophet (Zechariah 4:6),

"Not by might nor by power, but by My Spirit," says the LORD of hosts.

None of us stands before Him with anything to recommend us, and there is nothing that gets anyone to the front of the line.

Third, what is at stake is the truth that the Holy Spirit is both holy and spirit and cannot be manipulated by the earthly. In an absurd and—unless I am forgiven the triteness—irreverent comparison that will be understood by animal lovers, I have heard it said of cats that you cannot adopt a cat; if you are lucky, the cat adopts you. So it is with the Holy Spirit. We can do nothing to make Him anoint us with His presence and power; it is all a matter of His grace: the lovely, splendid, eternal Cat—perhaps I should say Lion—adopts us on His own. We can present our hearts to Him, and ask, and wait in faith; that is a matter of preparation. But, in the end, His sovereignty bestows the anointing without regard to anything we might have or be.

Fourth, for Elisha to receive a payment in exchange for a healing would be to accept something close to a bribe. But by ignoring Naaman's chariots full of wealth, Elisha teaches us that the anointing is not for sale. A situation in the book of Acts underscores this. After Philip evangelizes Samaria, Peter and John arrive from Jerusalem to impart the anointing by laying hands on those who believe and are baptized. When a former magician, Simon, sees how the anointing affects people when the apostles lay hands on them (Acts 8:18-23),

> *He offered them money, saying, "Give me this power also, that anyone on whom I lay hands may receive the Holy Spirit."*
> *But Peter said to him, "Your money perish with you, because you thought that the gift of God could be purchased with money! You have neither part nor portion in this matter, for your heart is not right in the sight of God. Repent therefore."*

These explanations, however, best apply where there is a flawed motive, seeking to get the power of God with money or other influence. But the case seems different with Naaman who, after he is healed, and to show deep gratitude, wants to give Elisha an offering in thanksgiving (II Kings 5:15):

> *"Please take a gift from your servant."*

Paul in several places states the principle of reward for ministry. He promotes an offering for the poor Jewish believers in Jerusalem, saying that the believers in Rome have an obligation because the gospel came to them through Jews (Romans 15:27):

> *For if [you] Gentiles have been partakers of their spiritual*

things, [your] duty is also to minister to them in material
things.

Then, citing an Old Testament principle which he holds to be still valid in the New, Paul says that elders ought to be supported financially (I Timothy 5:17,18):

Let the elders who rule well be counted worthy of double honor,
especially those who labor in the word and doctrine. For the
Scripture says, "You shall not muzzle an ox while it treads
out the grain," and "The laborer is worthy of his wages."

Finally, Paul says about his own apostolic ministry that financial support is his right (I Corinthians 9:7-14):

Who ever goes to war at his own expense? Who plants a
vineyard and does not eat of its fruit? Or who tends a flock
and does not drink of the milk of the flock? ... If we have
sown spiritual things for you, is it a great thing if we reap your
material things? ... Do you not know that those who minister
the holy things eat of the things of the temple...? Even so the
Lord has commanded that those who preach the gospel should
live from the gospel.

With all this evidence supporting material reward for spiritual ministry in both the Old and New Testaments, why does Elisha refuse Naaman's gift? (II Kings 5:16)

But he said, "As the LORD lives, before whom I stand, I will
receive nothing." And he urged him to take it, but he refused.

Perhaps there is yet something in Naaman's heart which would disqualify his gift. The situation might be like Abraham with the King of Sodom. After Abraham (then Abram) rescues Lot—together with the people and goods of Sodom—from invaders (Genesis 14:21-23),

the king of Sodom said to Abram, "Give me the persons, and
take the goods for yourself." But Abram said to the king of
Sodom, "I have lifted my hand to the LORD, God Most
High, the Possessor of heaven and earth, that I will take
nothing, from a thread to a sandal strap, and that I will not

> *take anything that is yours, lest you should say, 'I have made*
> *Abram rich.'"*

Or perhaps Elisha, the prophet, is simply led of the Holy Spirit in a test of his faith. He refuses what might have been an attractive and legitimate means of supplying his needs for ministry, knowing that God is the provider and will Himself choose other means than the Syrian to provide for the man of God.

Returning to Paul and his teaching that support for ministers is right and deserved, it is interesting that he continues (I Corinthians 9:15,18),

> *But I have used none of these things, nor have I written these*
> *things that it should be done so to me… What is my reward*
> *then? That when I preach the gospel, I may present the gospel*
> *of Christ without charge.*

Paul, although he has a right to expect a reward from the Corinthians for his ministry among them, is led by a higher motive to decline any material reward. Neither Paul nor Elisha minister in the anointing to make money. It would be legitimate if they had made money—and there are times when they do; but by refusing reward, they place ministry in a category beyond financial gain, and they pass the test of obedience and humility.

By contrast, this matter of money becomes a failed test for Gehazi, Elisha's servant. Instead of following Elisha's example when he says, *"As the* LORD *lives… I will take nothing,"* Gehazi says the opposite (II Kings 5:20),

> *"As the* LORD *lives, I will…take something."*

Large ministries with vast cash flows that attract attention and admiration might learn from this story. The anointing is about ministry—not about financial gain. Paul warns Timothy about people who are (I Timothy 6:5)

> *of corrupt minds and destitute of the truth, who suppose that*
> *godliness is a means of gain.*

Paul goes on to say that godliness with contentment is true gain, and that a modest lifestyle is preferable to wealth (v. 8-10):

And having food and clothing, with these we shall be content. But those who desire to be rich fall into temptation and a snare.... For the love of money is a root of all kinds of evil, for which some have strayed from the faith in their greediness, and pierced themselves through with many sorrows.

Gehazi's desire for wealth certainly brings him pangs: the sad result of his seeking the financial rewards of ministry is that he is cursed (II Kings 5:27):

"Therefore the leprosy of Naaman shall cling to you and your descendants forever." And he went out from his presence leprous, as white as snow.

Let this be a lesson to those today who are blessed with a powerful anointing that produces a following: greed is greed and brings a curse on the greedy—even as they bless others with the power of God.

7

THE SONS OF THE PROPHETS II

Loss of the anointing

The story of the axe head offers several principles of the anointing—symbolized in the details of loss and recovery. The plot begins as the sons of the prophets ask Elisha for his permission to build a new, larger headquarters. While felling a tree for a beam to be used in the construction, one of the men loses the head of the axe he is wielding, and it falls into the Jordan River (II Kings 6:5):

> *And he cried out and said, "Alas, master! For it was borrowed."*

We see that the work the men are about is good; it is needed and has the approval of the leadership. But something goes wrong. In the normal process of doing the work, one man loses the power to carry out his part of the job. As human strength cannot fell trees without applying a tool, so human ability cannot do the work of God without applying the anointing. And there are times when, having once had power, we may lose the ability to move in the anointing.

The anointing borrowed

When the man loses the axe head, and laments that it was borrowed, it reminds us about the anointing—that it, too, is borrowed. The anointing never is our own to use or abuse—or lose. It always is on loan to us from the heart of God.

To lose the manifest presence and power of God is indeed a great loss. To be reduced to natural experience and natural means, when we have once known the supernatural, is bereavement. The personal tragedy of lost power, however, is only part of the problem. There is also the loss to those who miss out on the benefit of what we would otherwise accomplish through the anointing. Since ministry is not about personal fulfillment so much as it is about fulfilling God's redemptive purposes through us, when we lose the anointing people around us suffer the loss of true ministry.

But the greatest loss has to do with the fact that we are, at best, stewards of the anointing entrusted to us by Another. The source of the anointing is God's Spirit, and mishandling the divine gift means that we have become unfaithful stewards of what He has provided.

One Bible figure well known for losing the anointing is Samson. Blessed by an angelic prophecy from before his birth, Samson's career displaying supernatural physical strength begins when (Judges 13:25)

The Spirit of the LORD began to move upon him.

And several more times the book of Judges records (14:6 and v.19; and 15:14),

The Spirit of the LORD came mightily upon him.

But one day Samson compromises the anointing by revealing to Delilah the secret of his Nazarite vow—and the importance of his long hair. When she waits until he is asleep and cuts off his hair, Scripture describes the sad result (Judges 16:20):

He did not know that the LORD had departed from him.

Without the anointing, Samson is an ordinary man of whom the Philistines take full advantage by gouging out his eyes and putting him to hard labor in prison.

The end of Samson's story—that his hair grows back and God restores his supernatural strength to pull down the Philistine temple and to kill thousands of Philistines and himself—is bittersweet. Although he has one final victory, it is amid the pathetic spectacle of a man of God, blinded, shackled and mocked by a carousing pagan mob. The loss of the anointing becomes for

Samson a fatal disgrace.

An important word in the story of the lost axe head is the lament, "Alas!" Alas for the lost power! Alas for the disgrace! Alas for the betrayed trust! Alas for the work unfinished! Alas for the comrades burdened! And so it is when the anointing is missing.

Not all interrupted ministry is the result of lost anointing. There are times when God sets His servants apart for a rest, or a change of direction, or to await a timely opportunity. Jesus says to His disciples, when they have successfully been casting out demons and healing the sick (Mark 6:31),

> *"Come aside by yourselves to a deserted place and rest a while." (For there were many coming and going, and they did not even have time to eat.)*

A break in the pattern or intensity of ministry can be vital to its usefulness, and wise is the servant of God who submits to the "time out."

But a loss of the anointing itself is devastating, because without the anointing, nothing worthwhile remains. Jesus says (John 15:5),

> *"Without Me you can do nothing."*

This is another way of saying that the anointing—His presence and power—is essential to all godly living, let alone a specific ministry.

When he is repenting of the sin with Bathsheba, David pleads with God (Psalm 51:11),

> *Do not take Your Holy Spirit from me.*

David understands the true issue: he does not ask that the kingdom not be taken from him, or that his life not be taken from him. The most important thing to David is the inner power of the Holy Spirit; take away anything else and it will be what he reckons he deserves, but take away the anointing and he is ruined.

The anointing restored

Continuing the picture of the lost axe head as a likeness of lost anointing, we see that what Elisha does is essential to restoration (II Kings 6:6):

And the man of God said, "Where did it fall?"

Sometimes we cannot go on until we go back, and so Elisha requires the man to go back and find the place of loss. When the anointing is lost, it is possible to identify the time and place. At least there is a point at which we become aware that the power is missing, and from there we are able to determine the cause. I have heard the story of a preacher counseling a person who was weeping over the lost sense of fellowship with God. "What is the reason?" the preacher asked. "I just don't know," was the tearful reply. "Well," the preacher advised, "take a good guess." In other words, we really do know in our heart the cause of the loss of anointing; it is likely the first thing that comes to mind. God meets us at our point of honesty; and our only hope of restoration is the honesty of soul that will confront the issue.

Sometimes the issue is carelessness—like Martha, simply being preoccupied with other things. Sometimes the issue is compromise—allowing our spiritual integrity to be violated by some decision, when we know God is leading otherwise. The issue may be moral—becoming hardened through the deceitfulness of sin. Or the issue may be bitterness and unforgiveness—allowing the words or actions of others to poison our spirit with resentment.

"Where did it fall?" Where did the loss of the anointing occur? This is the place to expect restoration (II Kings 6:6):

And he showed him the place. So he cut off a stick, and threw it in there; and he made the iron float.

The stick, like the salt in a previous story, symbolizes—indeed carries— the anointing. For reasons beyond logic, the power of God attaches to a simple stick and it causes a miracle as the iron axe head floats. The principle to see here, at least in part, is that only the anointing can restore anointing. Restoration involves the honesty of confessing the place of loss, but confession in itself is not enough. The anointing is such a supernatural phenomenon that nothing short of the supernatural can deal on its terms.

To illustrate in a different way, our family lived, for a number of years when our children were small, in an old farmhouse that had its own well. But the water pump in the basement was old and leaky and often lost pressure. Then it would grind away noisily, producing nothing but air. The way to get it going again was to pour a quantity of water down the pipe to "prime" it. Then the pump would regain its suction and begin to draw water up from deep in the earth. It needed water to restore the flow of water.

And we need the anointing to restore the flow of anointing. The human spirit needs to be primed by the Holy Spirit to flow in the Holy Spirit. Without an impartation of the Holy Spirit, no amount of doctrine or commitment or even remorse can release the supernatural flow.

The anointing and the Cross

I hope what I suggest next is not too strained a figure, but I see in the stick a hint of what completes the principle of restoration. I see that besides carrying the anointing, perhaps the stick can represent the Cross. There is no confusion here, and we need not ask which is meant—the anointing or the Cross, because the connection between the two is intrinsic. First, the atonement of the Cross works through the anointing. (Hebrews 9:14):

> *Christ…through the eternal Spirit offered Himself.*

Likewise, the anointing works because of the Cross (Ephesians 2:13,18):

> *But now in Christ Jesus you who once were far off have been made near by the blood of Christ…for through Him we both have access by one Spirit to the Father.*

The offering of Christ on the Cross is accomplished through the Holy Spirit, and the effect of the Cross makes the Holy Spirit available. Or we could say that, on the one hand, the power of the blood of Jesus comes to us by the anointing; and on the other hand, the anointing is released in us through the saving power of the blood.

At any rate, if the story of the axe head lost and restored is useful as a picture of anointing lost and restored, we do well to understand, from a New Testament perspective, that restoration comes at a price. The Cross is the stick thrown into the dark waters of loss; the axe head of the anointing rises and power is restored.

Grace is what both the anointing and the atonement have in common. That there is anointing to be experienced at all is due simply to the grace of a loving God whose desire is to share with us the goodness of His heart. And that there is forgiveness and restoration when we have done something to forfeit the precious anointing also is due to grace. Impartation and restoration spring from the same source. If we understand ourselves at all, we know that we do not deserve to receive God's power to begin with; and we deserve even less the patient ministry of the Holy Spirit to give us again the treasure we have mishandled. Grace, by definition, is for the undeserving.

Taking back the anointing

God does His part by making the axe head float. But something remains to be done (II Kings 6:7):

> Therefore [Elisha] said, "Pick it up for yourself." So he reached out his hand and took it.

Elisha knows what he is talking about, because he has been in a similar situation, having had to take up the mantle fallen from Elijah to carry on the prophetic ministry. Likewise, this son of the prophets must take up the floating axe head in order to continue his work.

As a picture of anointed ministry lost and restored, the axe head story would not be complete without this final scene in which the miracle of restoration is personalized. The man might be fearful of receiving the axe head again, since he has not used it well to begin with. He might make excuses about not being very good at axe wielding. He might try to hand off his responsibility to others who can show themselves more faithful. But what he needs to do is forget the past, forget what people think of him, forget his fear of failure, and reach for the axe head.

The message here is about faith—not so much to see the miracle, because it takes no faith for a man to witness a miracle of God's power; it is there before his eyes, floating on the surface of the water. But it takes faith to see himself restored to the anointing as a result of the miracle—faith to overcome shame and self-doubt. Instead of protesting unworthiness, the only useful thing to do is to believe that grace will restore the forfeited ministry, and to begin once again serving others in the anointing.

Faith and restoration

The question may arise, Is it really true that the anointing can be lost? Paul's words about gifts in Romans 11:29,

The gifts and the calling of God are irrevocable,

seem to suggest otherwise. But we know both through Scripture and by experience that loss of holy power is all too possible. The answer is in the way obedient faith enters the power equation. In Romans 11 Paul describes the condition of religious Jews who through unbelief fail to inherit the covenant relationship of their fathers. Paul has previously explained the cause of their loss—as contrasted with believing Gentiles (Romans 9:30-32):

> *Gentiles…have attained to righteousness, even the*
> *righteousness of faith; but Israel…has not attained to the law*
> *of righteousness. Why? Because they did not seek it by faith.*

A covenant relationship with God is there to be had by the Jews, because God's gifts and calling are irrevocable. But many Jews forfeit the covenant through lack of faith.

In the same way, we can forfeit the flow of anointing. To His disciples Jesus gives (Matthew 10:1) *power over unclean spirits, to cast them out, and to heal all kinds of sickness and all kinds of disease.*

But later, a disappointed father brings his epileptic son to Jesus, explaining that he has earlier brought him to the disciples (Matthew 17:16),

"But they could not cure him."

After Jesus successfully rebukes and casts out a demon of epilepsy, the disciples ask why they could not cast it out. Jesus replies (verse 20),

"Because of your unbelief...."

He has already given them all the power—the anointing—that they need, but they fail to engage it for lack of faith. The disciples would have done well to learn from Elisha and the son of the prophets the principle   of

returning to the place where the power was lost, and repenting of whatever had blocked their faith. In a follow-up comment, Jesus gives them a hint about recovering their faith (verse 21),

"However, this kind does not go out except by prayer and fasting."

Since prayer and fasting are all about enhancing faith to know God and to do His will, Jesus may be telling the disciples that they have neglected their relationship with God. If they would spend more time with Him in order to keep the anointing flowing through faith, they would be continually graced in the supernatural power of the Holy Spirit.

When we sense a lack of power we must first ask, Where in my life did the loss occur? Next we need to apply to the failure the grace of the Cross of Jesus Christ. And finally we need boldly to take up once again the anointing and use it for the glory of God and for the blessing of others and ourselves.

8

SYRIA

Supernatural vision

The king of Syria is frustrated: every time he plans an attack or an ambush against Israel, they find out about it. He can never take them by surprise, and he wants to know who is leaking classified military information. One of his aides has the answer (II Kings 6:12):

> *"Elisha, the prophet who is in Israel, tells the king of Israel the words that you speak in your bedroom."*

Elisha is not present to hear discussions in the Syrian royal council chamber, but he knows what is said there. This is quite an amazing phenomenon, and perfectly legitimate—it is neither fortune telling nor mind reading, but rather the prophetic manifestation called in the New Testament (I Corinthians 12:8) the *word of knowledge*. He receives through the Holy Spirit information not naturally known, revealed for God's purposes.

This prophetic experience is an interesting introduction to what happens next. The Syrian king decides to besiege the city of Dothan at night to capture Elisha who is living there. In the morning, Elisha's servant is frightened when he discovers that an army surrounds the city. But Elisha shows no alarm; in fact, he talks strangely of the Syrians actually being outnumbered (II Kings 6:16):

> *So he answered, "Do not fear, for those who are with us are more than those who are with them."*

These words must sound like madness to the servant, who can see perfectly well that the Syrians have overwhelming force. "Open your eyes, sir!" he might want to say. "The evidence is clear that we are doomed." But Elisha, who hears what cannot be heard naturally, also sees what cannot be seen naturally (v.17):

> Then Elisha prayed and said, "LORD, I pray, open his eyes that he may see." Then the LORD opened the eyes of the young man, and he saw. And behold, the mountain was full of horses and chariots of fire all around Elisha.

Elisha is serene in threatening circumstances, not because he follows a doctrine of faith, but because he sees the unseen realm. The anointing opens up to Elisha a realm that is more real than the natural. The Syrian army is really there. But the fiery army is even more really there—and more significant.

There is an important distinction, not always understood by the people of God, between an attempt to claim something by faith, and the revelation through the anointing. Elisha doesn't need to conjure up otherworldliness; he lives in such an abundance of the anointing that the supernatural realm is revealed to him. We call it *supernatural* only because our natural experience is generally so out of touch with that realm. But the anointing puts us back in touch with what has been there all along, and which we need not attempt to create by faith.

In His earthly ministry, Jesus Himself depends on a revelation of the more-real reality to do the things He does (John 5:19):

> "Most assuredly, I say to you, the Son can do nothing of Himself, but what He sees the Father do."

Because Jesus can see the Father in action in the unseen realm, He knows what to do. Another way of describing the way Jesus experiences supernatural ministry is (Luke 5:17),

> The power of the Lord was present to heal them.

Seeing the Father in action, and experiencing the presence of the power of the Lord, are essentially the same things. Remember that Jesus describes the anointing as His source of supernatural power (Luke 4:18,19). We can understand, then, that the anointing involves seeing the unseen realm (or becoming aware of spiritual reality) and experiencing the presence and power of God.

If we revisit Paul's words in II Corinthians 4:18,

> *We do not look at the things which are seen, but at the things which are not seen. For the things which are seen are temporary, but the things which are not seen are eternal,*

we understand that this passage repeats the theme that there is another realm different from the ordinary visible realm. It adds that the invisible realm is more worth looking at than the visible because it is eternal. With eternity in our hearts—the deep longing of every human soul—we are better served by an awareness of the real-but-invisible spirit realm than by natural sight in the natural world if for no better reason than that it is infinitely bigger and lasts forever.

When Paul says, "We...look," he seems to be talking about something a little different from what is described in the story about Elisha's servant seeing two armies. In the story, the servant sees at first an army in the natural visible realm. But then his eyes are opened to the otherwise invisible but real—and really-there-all-along—spirit realm. And he sees another army, all fiery and supernaturally powerful, outnumbering the natural army. It is not a subjective pious delusion, but rather something really there that he actually sees. Paul, on the other hand, is not necessarily saying that we always see something when "we...look." Rather, we have an awareness of the spirit realm. Nevertheless, it is the same realm—the Heavenly spiritual realm accessible by the anointing—that Elisha, Elisha's servant and Paul all experience.

This truth of another realm that is more real than the natural realm is essential to understanding spiritual things in general, and the anointing in particular. It is especially useful to realize that the other realm is right here right now, though out of focus, as it were. When we talk about the anointing, we are really describing the invisible realm brought into focus. Heaven touches earth. God touches man. The oil of the Holy Spirit is applied and our spirit becomes involved in real and wonderful things that cannot be explained naturally. What is going on in the spiritual realm is more than we can see naturally, but the presence and power of God are available to us by the miracle of the anointing.

Supernatural blindness

By an ironic twist, in the same story in which Elisha prays for his servant to see, he also prays the opposite—that men might not see. The Syrian army threatening the prophet finds itself suddenly helpless (II Kings 6:18):

> *So when the Syrians came down to him, Elisha prayed to the LORD, and said, "Strike this people, I pray, with blindness." So He struck them with blindness.*

Later, when Elisha leads the blind army into the well-armed capital city of Samaria, he applies the anointing to reverse the blindness (v. 20):

> *So it was, when they had come to Samaria, that Elisha said, "LORD, open the eyes of these men, that they may see." And the LORD opened their eyes, and they saw.*

This can be a useful picture for us of spiritual blindness and spiritual sight, especially regarding the detail that the same power can have negative as well as positive effect on spiritual perception. When Saul of Tarsus, en route to Damascus to arrest believers in Jesus, is himself arrested by a light from Heaven and the voice of Jesus calling him to faith and service, he experiences first blindness and then restored vision (Acts 9:8,17-18):

> *Then Saul arose from the ground, and when his eyes were opened, he saw no one. But they led him by the hand and brought him into Damascus.... And Ananias went his way and entered the house; and laying his hands on him he said, "Brother Saul, the Lord Jesus, who appeared to you on the road as you came, has sent me that you may receive your sight and be filled with the Holy Spirit." Immediately there fell from his eyes something like scales, and he received his sight.*

Notice that it is the power of the Lord that both blinds Saul and gives him sight. Meanwhile, his calling to the gospel ministry—that comes while he is yet blind in Damascus—is that he is (Acts 26:18)

> *to open their eyes and to turn them from darkness to light, and from the power of Satan to God, that they may receive forgiveness of sins and an inheritance among those who are sanctified by faith in Me.*

This restoration of spiritual sight remains a passion for Paul the apostle who many years later prays for believers that (Ephesians 1:18)

> *the eyes of your understanding being enlightened...you may know what is the hope of His calling, what are the riches of the glory of His inheritance in the saints.*

When Jesus begins to use parables in His teaching, the disciples ask Him (Matthew 13:10),

> *"Why do you speak to them in parables?"*

A popular, but mistaken, idea is that Jesus, being the Master Teacher, uses stories and examples of ordinary people and objects and situations to illustrate truth for the masses. Exactly the opposite is the case, as Jesus Himself explains (vv.11-16),

> *"Because it has been given to you to know the mysteries of the kingdom of heaven, but to them it has not been given.... Therefore I speak to them in parables, because seeing they do not see, and hearing they do not hear, nor do they understand.... But blessed are your eyes for they see."*

Parables, meaning "dark sayings," are actually intended to do two things: reveal truth and conceal it—at the same time. For those with spiritual enlightenment, truth is revealed by the stories Jesus tells. But for those with unenlightened hearts, the darkness just increases. This arrangement—at first consideration—seems unfair. But Jesus has His reason, and it has to do with the anointing. Those who are willing to receive the anointing are given spiritual sight, whereas those without anointing are without it by choice, and it is impossible for them to understand because it is a supernatural message. In His words to the Laodicean church, the glorious Christ says (Revelation 3:17,18),

> *"Because you say, 'I am rich...and have need of nothing,'--
> and do not know that you are...blind..., I counsel you... to
> anoint your eyes with eye salve, that you may see."*

The sad fact is that even those in the church who have unanointed spiritual eyes often do not know it, and their blindness becomes for them a normal abnormality of deadly consequence. Jesus says of people who trust in their traditional interpretations of Scripture (Matthew 15:14),

> *"Let them alone. They are blind leaders of the blind. And if
> the blind leads the blind, both will fall into a ditch."*

A.W. Tozer, a preacher and author in the mid-Twentieth Century, regarded by many as a prophetic voice to the church at large, has said, "When all the evidence is in it may well be found that none but the proud ever strayed from the truth, and that self-trust was behind every heresy that ever afflicted the church." It is a solemn warning for us all to live in humble distrust of our natural understanding, and to seek constantly the anointing that alone can open our eyes. Because if we do not seek revelation by the anointing of the Spirit of truth, we will surely be cursed with blindness while we think we can see.

The prophet and the officer

In a later run-in with the Syrians, Samaria is besieged. The siege drags on as the Syrian army surrounds the capital city of Israel, and the famine conditions inside the walls have reached horrific proportions. Citizens of the city, rich and poor alike, are gaunt with starvation, and are desperate for a remedy. People are eating bird droppings just to survive. And the almost unthinkable—cannibalism—has begun.

Suddenly Elisha has a word from God that seems almost too good to be true (II Kings 7:1):

> *Then Elisha said, "Hear the word of the LORD. Thus says
> the LORD: 'Tomorrow about this time a seah of fine flour*

97

> *shall be sold for a shekel, and two seahs of barley for a shekel, at the gate of Samaria.'"*

Then one man says what many are thinking (II Kings 7:2):

> *So an officer on whose hand the king leaned answered the man of God and said, "Look, if the LORD would make windows in heaven, could this thing be?"*

Prophecy of an imminent end to a long siege sounds wonderful, but when frustration has tortured endurance beyond the breaking point, claims of change can seem hollow. The New Testament counsels us (I Thessalonians 5:20),

> *Do not despise prophecies,*

mainly because prophecies—in focusing on the unseen—tend to sound preposterous. To "despise" means here not so much to hate as to regard with scorn—to treat as unworthy. To the king's officer Elisha's words are simply unbelievable because he has no way of processing them logically. Day after day of starvation, with no hope in sight because of an entrenched and well-supplied enemy army laying siege, has been the experience not only of the officer but of the entire city. But when the anointing flows—when Heaven touches earth—and a message of miraculous hope comes, neither logic nor previous experience can be trusted to explain it.

The Lord says to Abraham, when Sarah laughs at news of a child to be born after her bearing years are long over (Genesis 18:14),

> *"Is anything too hard for the LORD?"*

The answer is, No—nothing is too hard for the Lord. He can do anything He wants to do. And He will do what He says He will do, regardless of difficulties that seem to be in the way.

The difference between the officer and the prophet is not that one is suffering and the other is prospering; they both are physically hungry. The difference is that the officer is looking at what can be seen, and the prophet is looking at what cannot be seen. The one sees the difficulties, but the other sees the deliverance. The one lives within a natural frame of reference, while the other lives in the anointing.

What follows seems a harsh judgment as Elisha calmly lowers this sentence upon the officer who doubts the prophetic word (II Kings 7:2):

> *"In fact, you shall see it with your eyes, but you shall not eat of it."*

To the unbeliever the prophecies of deliverance and of judgment sound equally foolish. But in a very brief time the truth of both is revealed.

Nothing to lose

The scene changes to outside the gates of Samaria where four lepers, outcast and destitute, strike up a conversation among themselves. They are figuring out that they have nothing to lose by going to the camp of the besieging Syrians in an attempt to survive, since they are dying of starvation anyway (II Kings 7:3,4):

> *And they said to one another, "Why are we sitting here until we die? If we say, 'We will enter the city,' the famine is in the city and we shall die there. And if we sit here, we die also. Now therefore, come, let us surrender to the army of the Syrians. If they keep us alive, we shall live; and if they kill us, we shall but die."*

The key point here is that they have nothing to lose. They are already outside the gates—and have been ever since their leprosy was diagnosed—and they have less between them and disaster than do those inside the city. So among all the citizens of Samaria only the lepers perceive that it would be better to die trying to live than to die trying to maintain a worthless sense of security a little longer. The others think that their hope is in shutting themselves behind the gates and presenting the appearance of strength. But apart from a miracle, they will die just as sure a death as the lepers.

As things would appear, the lepers have less than anyone else does—a situation to their advantage because it makes them free of pretension. There is a spiritual principle that those with the least to lose tend to be the first to be willing to receive blessing. Jesus teaches (Matthew 5:3),

> *"Blessed are the poor in spirit, for theirs is the kingdom of heaven,"*

by which He encourages an outlook of poverty rather than of riches—of weakness rather than strength—in order to gain the kingdom. And He specifically warns (Matthew 19:24),

> *"It is easier for a camel to go through the eye of a needle than for a rich man to enter the kingdom of God."*

These words come after a young rich man, who in fact senses a need in his life, asks Jesus what he should do to inherit the kingdom. When Jesus tells him to sell his possessions (v. 22),

> *He went away sorrowful, for he had great possessions.*

The bottom line for this young man is that he has something to lose, and he chooses to hold on to the apparent security of his riches, rather than let go in order to grasp the Kingdom instead.

The lepers are well-positioned because they know that they have nothing at all, and therefore have nothing to lose. Because of this, their story develops as an example of God's grace given to those desperate enough to take any risk (II Kings 7:5):

> *And they rose at twilight to go to the camp of the Syrians; and when they had come to the outskirts of the Syrian camp, to their surprise no one was there.*

God plays a trick on the enemy by making them hear sounds of another army advancing, so they flee, leaving everything behind. When the lepers explore one tent after another, they find to their astonishment so much food and drink and wealth that they fill themselves and carry away armloads to hiding.

The anointing—the power of God—does indeed open the windows of Heaven, releasing incalculable blessing. And the first to receive the benefit are the few who know they have nothing to lose.

Characteristics of a move of the Spirit

Perhaps every move of the Spirit of God is preceded by these several characteristics. First there is a spiritual famine (Amos 8:11,12):

"Behold, the days are coming," says the Lord GOD, "that I will send a famine on the land, not a famine of bread, nor a thirst for water, but of hearing the words of the LORD. They shall wander from sea to sea, and from north to east; they shall run to and fro, seeking the word of the LORD, but shall not find it."

When God's people become restless for reality, sensing that there is more for their hearts than the things they have been feeding on, there is hope for a move of God. Jesus says (Matthew 5:6),

"Blessed are those who hunger and thirst for righteousness, for they shall be filled."

Hunger precedes satisfaction. And until people are hungry, they will not seek something more.

But hunger itself is not enough. The lepers have the desperate boldness to take a risk. The great danger of orthodoxy—correct doctrine and traditional religion—is that believers can easily hide within their correctness, as behind the shut gates of a city, while they starve on the inside. It may take spiritual desperados, foolish enough to attempt the unheard-of, to discover the lavish renewed provision of grace in unexpected directions.

It took the foolishness of a German monk to stand against the conventional religion of his day and nail to the door of the church ninety-five scriptural convictions, launching the Reformation. It took the scandal of ordained Anglican clergymen to preach such a gospel of grace and holiness that they were put out of the official churches to preach in the fields and marketplaces, in the movement known as the Wesleyan Methodist revival. It took the garish sensationalism of brass bands and tambourines in the streets of cities around the world to attract the poor masses to the gospel through the Salvation Army. And throughout the Twentieth and into the Twenty-first Century, it is the risk-takers of each

101

generation who pioneer for the church in the fresh channels of the anointing.

In each move of the Holy Spirit, the reason things move is that the people who experience the Spirit give away what they have received. There is something irresistible about sharing a wonderful experience. Once the lepers enter into the experience, they find a message burning within themselves. The overwhelming experience of coming upon food and treasure in such abundance motivates them to tell others. They are like Elisha himself when he sees Elijah caught up in a whirlwind, and receives his mantle: Elisha leaves the scene of blessing to go back to the others with the anointing he now has. Amid the excitement of their discovery, the lepers say to each other (II Kings 7:9),

> *"We are not doing what is right. This day is a day of good news, and we remain silent. If we wait until morning light, punishment will come upon us. Now therefore, come, let us go and tell the king's household."*

What follows is another characteristic of a move of the Spirit of God: instead of receiving the testimony of discovered blessing, some of the people who need it the most are the most reluctant to embrace it. When the lepers return to the city and tell the gatekeepers their story, their message is carried to the palace where the reaction is doubt: the king assumes the whole thing is a trap. In other words, the leadership reacts instinctively with the idea that this can't be God blessing us; it must be the enemy tricking us.

One bold servant of the king is willing to sound unreasonable enough to suggest that the lepers might be right (II Kings 7:13):

> *And one of his servants answered and said, "Please…let us send… and see."*

He isn't interested in proving the report wrong; he wants to prove it right. This news, though hard to believe, is the only hope for the city. And it is at least worth a try. Thank God for people in every move of the Spirit who hear the strange reports of those who first experience the fresh anointing, and who say, "Maybe this is God. Maybe we should find out for ourselves before we dismiss this out of hand." After the king agrees to an investigation and the report of God's power is proven true, the news travels fast (II Kings 7:16):

> *Then the people went out and plundered the tents of the Syrians. So a seah of fine flour was sold for a shekel, and two seahs of barley for a shekel, according to the word of the* LORD.

Seeing is not experiencing

The news is not all good, however, because at least one man misses out on the blessing. He is the royal officer who had challenged the prophetic word of Elisha the day before. As it happens, the king appoints the officer to be in charge of the gate, and there, as the hungry people surge toward the promised blessing, he is trampled to death. Thus is fulfilled the prophesied judgment (vv.2, 19), "In fact, you shall see it with your eyes, but you shall not eat of it."

A final principle to gather from this story is that it is possible to witness a move of the Spirit of God but not experience it. Those who dismiss the anointing as irrelevant or deceptive, or who watch curiously or critically, place themselves in jeopardy so that the very thing which brings life to others brings death to them.

The Great Awakening, which influenced the American colonies in the mid-Eighteenth Century, had as its legacy many conversions, as well as the reviving of individual believers and whole congregations—often affecting entire communities. However, the move of the Spirit came at the price of much controversy as to whether it was of God. (Strange phenomena—people shaking and crying out and falling to the ground and having visions—accompanied the otherwise welcome increase in holy living and conversions and church attendance.) A major spokesman for the Awakening, Jonathan Edwards—a pastor and the founder of Princeton University—confronted doubters with these words in his *Distinguishing Marks of a Work of the Spirit of God,* first published in 1741:

> Those who stand wondering at this strange work, not
> knowing what to make of it, and refusing to receive it—and
> ready it may be sometimes to speak contemptibly of it, as
> was the case with the Jews of old—would do well to
> consider, and to tremble at St. Paul's words to them. Acts
> xiii.40, 41: "Beware therefore, lest that come upon you
> which is spoken of in the prophets, Behold, ye despisers,
> and wonder, and perish; for I work a work in your days,
> which you shall in no wise believe, though a man declare it
> unto you." Those who cannot believe the work to be true,
> because of the extraordinary degree and manner of it,
> should consider how it was with the unbelieving lord in
> Samaria, who said, "Behold, if the Lord should make
> windows in Heaven, might this thing be?" To whom Elisha
> said, "Behold, thou shall see it with thine eyes, but shalt not
> eat thereof."

Later in the same publication, Edwards adds this warning to people
who refuse to either accept or reject the work of the Holy Spirit:

> This pretended prudence, in persons waiting so long before
> they acknowledged this work, will probably in the end prove
> the greatest imprudence. Hereby they will fail of any share
> of so great a blessing, and will miss the most precious
> opportunity of obtaining divine light, grace, and comfort,
> Heavenly and eternal benefits that God ever gave to New
> England. While this glorious fountain is set open in so
> wonderful a manner, and multitudes flock to it and receive a
> rich supply for the wants of their souls, they stand at a
> distance, doubting, wondering, and receiving nothing, and
> are like to continue thus till the precious season is past.

What Jonathan Edwards warned of in his day can happen in
ours: conservative believers doubtful of any move of the Holy
Spirit where supernatural things happen. They can raise such
questions of propriety that God's sovereign stirrings are rejected
out of hand. Like the king in Samaria who distrusts reports of
abundant blessing, fearing a trick, Christians who hear of

miraculous goings-on can think the devil is behind the very work of God. The dangerous position they are in when they thus call good evil may be what Jesus warns of when He says (Matthew 12:32),

> *"Whoever speaks against the Holy Spirit, it will not be forgiven him, either in this age or in the age to come."*

A solemn warning, this. Of course there will be things to criticize in the behavior of people in any move of the Holy Spirit—every revival has excesses that need discerning correction. People may do things to attract attention, or they may copy others who have a true experience, or they may be used of the enemy to detract from the rest of what God is doing. But for believers to assume that strange reports of unusual blessing mean that it is all a counterfeit and a trick of the devil may bring fearful consequences. Whether or not this is an unpardonable sin, what is certain is that the critics who reject the work of the Holy Spirit miss out on the abundant flow of the goodness of God that the anointing brings.

How much wiser the servant who suggests, "Let us send and see." He understands that discernment is impossible if phenomenal reports are not even tested. He is hungry enough to believe that God may have opened a source of blessing beyond all expectation. He is willing to step outside of the perceived safety of the walls on the chance that a source of life will be found to deliver many people from starvation and defeat.

May such voices be heard in our day, calling God's people beyond their trusted tradition to seek out the anointing in the hope of experiencing reviving grace that may be waiting just a few bold steps away.

9

THE SHUNAMMITE II

Timing of the Spirit

II Kings 8 revisits the story of the Shunammite woman and her son, adding several more principles of the anointing for us to see. As the chapter begins, Elisha tells the woman to depart with her family to another land to escape a coming famine in Israel. One thing to notice is that God does not abandon later the people He touches with His anointing early on. The Shunammite family, having experienced the powerful touch of God—first by a supernatural birth and then by a resurrection—are not just material for one more story in the Bible. They are real people whose encounter with the real God is ongoing. He does not love and leave; He is always faithful. The Shunammite woman has shown her hunger for God and His blessing in her life, and God has already given her more than she could ask or think. And with a new emergency there comes a new release of anointing. The man of God brings a prophetic word designed to save the lives—and the prosperity—of the woman and her family.

For seven years the family stays safely in exile, and then returns home. But now they have a further problem: they find that squatters have taken over their abandoned property. So the Shunammite goes with her son to the king to appeal for her house and land to be restored.

It is the next detail that shows a feature of the Holy Spirit's work—the exquisite timing of events that display God's love and power (II Kings 8:4,5):

> *Then the king talked with Gehazi, the servant of the man of God, saying, "Tell me, please, all the great things Elisha has done." Now it happened, as he was telling the king how he*

had restored the dead to life, that there was the woman whose son he had restored to life, appealing to the king for her house and for her land. And Gehazi said, "My lord, O king, this is the woman, and this is her son whom Elisha restored to life."

The emergency in the woman's life and the curiosity in the king's heart coincide in a way that benefits both and suggests that the Spirit of God has arranged the timing. In a single event, the woman has a favorable introduction to the king, and the king has Gehazi's story of the miracle confirmed. Although Elisha is not present for this timely crossing of paths, the mark of his anointing is all over it. These people associated with Elisha find their lives strangely intersecting with one another in a gracious coincidence.

Anointing spreads its blessing as divine appointments unfold around people who move in the power of God. The Bible is full of such timely miracles. Abraham's servant is sovereignly led to Rebekah as a wife for Isaac as she comes to draw water (Genesis 24); Saul's donkeys are lost and he goes to Samuel the seer for help as Samuel is looking for him to anoint him king (I Samuel 9); godly Mordecai's jealous enemy, Haman, visits the palace, ironically at the hour the king decides to have someone publicly honor Mordecai as a reward for loyal service (Esther 6); God prepares a great fish to swallow the prophet Jonah at the moment he is thrown overboard (Jonah 1:17); Jesus sends two disciples into Jerusalem with instructions to encounter a man carrying a pitcher of water and to follow him to a house where a room is already prepared for the last supper (Mark 14); Peter has a vision instructing him not to call unclean what God has called clean just before "unclean" Gentiles arrive from Cornelius, seeking the truth of the gospel (Acts 10).

In all of these stories, and more, in the Bible and throughout church history, there is an amazing timeliness of events that points to the power of God's Spirit at work on behalf of those in touch with Him.

The King's agent

The Shunammite has in mind a simple principle of justice when she appeals to the king. She wants her house and land back. Already her connection with Elisha's anointing and the miracles he has done have provided her with unexpected favor. But the king not only is pleased to meet her, he is willing to do two things beyond what she asks. First, he appoints an officer for her—an official with the authority to see that she is taken care of. She is not left with just the good word of the king, although the king's word is necessary as the legal basis for receiving righteous favor. The king foresees that the Shunammite will need help; he does not expect her to be able to get what she needs by herself. She will not be alone to face either the issues or the opposition that lie ahead. Nor has she anything to fear in the officer, because the king charges him with her welfare. How impressive for the Shunammite as she returns home, not only with a favorable decision from the throne, but personally accompanied by the officer of the king appointed to see that everything is carried out as decreed!

The Holy Spirit is our officer to care for us. He is the One given to us by the Father through Jesus to come alongside us to help, as Jesus explains (John 14:16):

> *"And I will pray the Father, and He will give you another Helper, that He may abide with you forever."*

We are not left with simply the Word of the King, although the Word is necessary and absolute. But we have been given the King's own agent. He is not to be feared, because He has been given to us for our good, and He represents the King's will in bringing about the fulfillment of His purposes for us. As Jesus says again (John 16:13-15),

> *He will not speak on His own authority, but whatever He hears He will speak.... He will take of what is Mine, and declare it to you. All things that the Father has are Mine.*

The plan is not that we are to figure out how to live in the favor of the King. We are not expected to establish ourselves, any more than the Shunammite was expected to take the king's decree home by herself. We can relax in the care of the Holy Spirit who is sent by the authority of the King.

The Holy Spirit's authority is in the anointing. The anointing flows from the throne and is more than legal right—it is power. Paul reminds the Thessalonians (I Thessalonians 1:5),

> *For our gospel did not come to you in word only, but also in power, and in the Holy Spirit.*

If the gospel comes in word only, it is doctrinal only—ideas to be believed. But the gospel that comes with the Holy Spirit and power is a force to be engaged. Hearts and minds are actually changed, hopeless circumstances are unraveled, bodies are healed, and material provision is supplied not by Bible verses alone, but by the invasive anointing.

Jesus (Luke 4:14)

> *returned in the power of the Spirit to Galilee,*

and in that power He preached the Kingdom of God and taught such things as people had never before heard. But also in that power, He turned water to wine, healed the sick, raised the dead, walked on water, fed lunch to thousands, and calmed stormy weather, among other things. Words plus power. The Holy Spirit was with Jesus and the anointing flowed through Him as a result.

Redemptive abundance

The second thing the king of Israel does for the Shunammite woman, besides granting the return of her land through the authority of his officer, is to restore, as well (II Kings 8:6),

> *"all the proceeds of the field from the day that she left the land until now."*

This is good news, indeed! Restoration is made in the most complete sense, because it is not just a former possession now reclaimed, it goes back in time to claim what has not yet been possessed. This is a redemptive stroke similar to the promise to Israel through the prophet Joel (2:25):

*So I will restore to you the years that the swarming locust has
eaten, the crawling locust, the consuming locust, and the
chewing locust.*

God is promising not only to remove the locusts from the land, but
by His power to make up for the loss of all the crops destroyed by
the locusts through the years. This is the more-than-expected and
more-than-deserved way that the redemptive power of the
anointing works to reverse curses and losses. Much is lost by the
ravages of circumstances beyond our control, and by the
destructive work of our enemy, a thief who, like the locusts (John
10:10),

does not come except to steal, and to kill, and to destroy.

But when our King restores, it is to a degree that exceeds
imagination (Ephesians 3:20):

*Now to Him who is able to do exceedingly abundantly beyond
all that we ask or think, according to the power that works in
us, to Him be glory in the church by Christ Jesus throughout
all ages, world without end. Amen.*

The abundance is clearly linked to "the power that works in us"—
precisely the definition of the anointing.

10

THE PROPHECIES

Continuity of ministry

The next stories of frustrated prophecies present a problem. Perhaps the fact that there are complications is actually good; we need to be reminded that the anointing is not something to understand altogether. But I offer here some thoughts that may be helpful.

The history behind these prophecies—and their connection with Elisha—starts with Elijah. Near the end of Elijah's prophetic career, God tells him to anoint three men (I Kings 19:15,16):

> Then the LORD said to him: "Go...anoint Hazael as king over Syria. Also you shall anoint Jehu...as king over Israel. And Elisha...you shall anoint as prophet in your place."

Two kings and a prophet are to be anointed. But there is no record that Elijah ever anoints any of them—not, at least, with literal oil in the usual manner. Nor is there any record of any dealings of Elijah at all after this with either Hazael or Jehu, the two who are named to be kings, but only with Elisha, Elijah's successor as prophet. (Although any pouring of literal oil on him is not in the story, the spiritual anointing passed on to Elisha is foundational to this book.)

Why doesn't Elijah anoint Hazael and Jehu, as the Lord in a prophetic revelation tells him? I think the answer may be that since there is a continuity of ministry to his successor, the instructions given to Elijah about anointing kings is passed on to Elisha for fulfillment. Elijah may know that for his own ministry the timing to anoint the kings is wrong, and that the task will properly fall to Elisha in days to come.

This theme of delayed ministry, where the sense of vision

and calling is passed to a successor appears several times in Scripture. Moses does not get to lead Israel into the Promised Land; the ministry of leadership is passed to Joshua. David does not get to build the temple; the project goes to Solomon instead. And even Jesus' ministry is passed on in two phases or levels. First, He passes on to the Holy Spirit His ministry of teaching the disciples (John 16:7,12,13):

> *"Nevertheless I tell you the truth. It is to your advantage that I go away; for if I do not go away, the Helper will not come to you…I still have many things to say to you, but you cannot bear them now. However, when He, the Spirit of truth, has come He will guide you into all truth."*

Second, Jesus passes on to believers the ministry of powerful works. The work of believers is to be a continuation of His work (John 14:12):

> *"Most assuredly, I say to you, he who believes in Me, the works that I do he will do also; and greater works than these he will do."*

There is a continuity of the anointing in the delay. Even Jesus in His earthly ministry does not do everything that needs to be done. The Holy Spirit comes to take Jesus' followers even further than He does; and they are thus prepared to continue His Kingdom work. The book of Acts, documenting the coming of the Holy Spirit, the launching of the church, and the empowering of the apostles, begins by referring to (Acts 1:1)

> *all that Jesus began both to do and teach.*

This clearly suggests that Jesus' work is only a beginning. The work goes on because of the continuity of the anointing; the Holy Spirit who empowers Jesus also empowers the church.

This principle of delayed ministry is key to understanding the anointing, because it removes the emphasis from an individual's accomplishment to the larger accomplishment of God's purposes through the Spirit. Not that we can overemphasize the ministry of Jesus, but we might so value the earthly events of His ministry that we fail to see that what He does in His few years on earth is the product of the same anointing available to us.

This principle also applies to our own work. What we are called to do is never an end in itself, but always part of a transcending scheme. If we fail in a lifetime to accomplish all that is in our heart, we are not to think that we are a failure, because the Holy Spirit will continue anything He begins through us. It matters nothing to Heaven who of us begins or ends the work. Jesus explains this when He says (John 4:36-38),

> *"And he who reaps receives wages, and gathers fruit for eternal life, that both he who sows and he who reaps may rejoice together. For in this the saying is true: 'One sows, and another reaps.' I sent you to reap that for which you have not labored; others have labored, and you have entered into their labors."*

Paul, seeking to take attention away from individual ministers, says also (I Corinthians 3:5-8),

> *Who then is Paul, and who is Apollos, but ministers through whom you believed.... I planted, Apollos watered, but God gave the increase. So then neither he who plants is anything, nor he who waters, but God who gives the increase. Now he who plants and he who waters are one.*

The source of their unity is the anointing—and the Spirit that empowers them provides the continuity of the ministry. No one who ministers in the anointing need have any fear of being replaced or eclipsed by another, or of being a failure when the vision goes unfulfilled, because the ministry in the Spirit is larger than any individual minister.

Caution in anointing

And there is another issue. While Hazael and Jehu each, in fact, eventually becomes king of his respective country, only Jehu is first anointed with oil. (This is done by one of the sons of the prophets, at Elisha's command.) Is there a reason for this that has spiritual significance?

113

I think there is a possibility that Elisha wants to distance himself—and the authority implied in the act of applying the oil—from both the political intrigue of Syria as well as the evil that he sees that Hazael will inflict on Israel (II Kings 8:12):

> *"I know the evil that you will do to the children of Israel: their strongholds you will set on fire, and their young men you will kill with the sword; and you will dash their children, and rip open their women with child."*

Paul's advice to Timothy follows along these lines when he advises (I Timothy 5:22),

> *Do not lay hands upon any one hastily, nor share in other people's sins; keep yourself pure.*

This may refer to the words Paul has just written about protecting the integrity of local church government. Timothy is warned not to align with an elder whose sinful lifestyle disgraces the church.

In the Old Testament, the literal anointing of poured oil confers authority and can also confer spiritual power, as we have seen; in the New Testament the method of transferring spiritual anointing is instead by the laying on of hands. The message that the Old Testament prophet models, the New Testament apostle affirms: anointing is to be handled with caution and wisdom.

God's sovereignty and the anointing

I have saved for last the most difficult—in my opinion—of the issues in these stories of the kings. It is the strangely contradictory reply to the king of Syria who is ill and wants some prophetic encouragement. Hazael is sent by the king to inquire of Elisha (II Kings 8:9,10):

> *So Hazael went...and stood before him and said, "Your son Ben-Hadad king of Syria has sent me to you, saying, 'Shall I recover from this disease?'" And Elisha said to him, "Go, say to him, 'You shall certainly recover.' However, the LORD has shown me that he will really die."*

What happens is that Hazael returns to Ben-Hadad with the message that he will recover, but in fact the next day Hazael murders the king by smothering him (v.15),

so that he died; and Hazael reigned in his place.

To sort out the difficulties here, we need to look at each part of the story. To begin with, it is God's purpose for Hazael to become king of Syria. We don't know God's reason, but it is clear that He tells Elijah that he is to anoint Hazael as king, although it would appear that Elijah never does this.

Secondly, we have the current king of Syria, Ben-Hadad, ill and sending Hazael to inquire of the prophet Elisha about his recovery. Almost simultaneously, Elisha gets prophetic impressions from the Lord that Ben-Hadad will recover, but also that he will die. (And he also receives confirmation that Hazael will become king, succeeding Ben-Hadad, but that he will be very cruel.)

The question is how can Ben-Hadad both recover and die? Generally we all recover from illnesses—and one day each of us will die anyway. But the implication seems to be—and in fact it works out—that Ben-Hadad's dying will pre-empt his recovery. It would seem that the only answer is that it is God's intention that he should recover from the illness, but that calamity intervenes when Hazael murders him.

Is this possible—that God wills and even prophetically declares one thing, but that something else happens? Apparently so. I think that this question, which is essentially about our definition of God's sovereignty, is an important part of a discussion of the anointing.

God's sovereignty is about His kingly authority; and the anointing is about His power. Authority and power clearly relate, but perhaps an understanding of how they relate is not always clear. For example, the idea that God's sovereignty means that God has fixed the outcome of all events from His eternal perspective suggests an almost fatalistic view of history: whatever will be will be. It might be thought that since nothing can happen outside of either God's will or God's knowledge, then—because nothing can

115

contradict His will and because God already knows the future—everything that happens is pre-programmed, as it were. Or, to put it another way, as I heard a preacher say once, we are on a track the whole time—and only think we are steering. By this thinking, all life circumstances—births, and accidents, and illnesses, and fortunes gained and lost—all are more or less like something cast in concrete, rather than something fluid and changeable.

These things are difficult to prove or disprove. But one of the consequences of holding this view of the sovereignty of God is the impression it can convey that there is no reason to seek God's manifest power flowing into our circumstances, because He has already decreed the outcome.

Related to this thinking is the idea that since we have the Bible, the written Word of God that is (Psalm 119:89)

forever...settled in heaven,

to seek anything more is to insult the Word. If we accept such a notion, then to experience God's power becomes irrelevant, because what we need is knowledge of the Bible rather than an experience. If the Bible tells us that God is loving, for instance, then there is no need to experience divine love. Prophetic direction—words spoken by a supernatural gift—are unnecessary for us, because we have the Bible stories of how God speaks to His people in olden times. He needs to speak to them prophetically because they do not have the Bible, but since we have the stories we don't need the prophecy.

There is an odd logic here, however, that we might well challenge. If we are supposed to learn from the Bible, why is it inappropriate to allow the Bible to lead us to experience God's presence and power in ways similar to how the people in the Bible experience Him? Or—more to our point—why should we not assume that by our cooperation with God's will we can experience the anointing flowing in us to bring about the fulfillment of His will?

Hazael might have trusted the anointing—the power of God—to elevate him to the throne in due time. If he had cooperated with God's power, rather than asserting his own, he still would have entered into the sovereign will of God that he become king, but he would have avoided murder and would not have violated whatever God's purpose was for Ben-Hadad's recovery. Besides this, it may be that by his act of violence in murdering the king he opens the door to the evil influence that Elisha prophetically sees as characterizing Hazael's reign.

My thought here is that the anointing is dynamic by definition and that it is as possible to quench the Spirit as to yield to Him. We may hold an inaccurate view of God when we think of His sovereignty as a force that cannot be stopped or a purpose that cannot be changed. God will have His way in the end, but we will share in the fulfillment of His will to the extent that we cooperate with His loving, holy, truthful character in a supernatural flow of the Holy Spirit.

Prophetic emotions

A further thing to learn from this story of Hazael's encounter with Elisha is in the incidental details of Elisha's experience of the prophetic anointing. Not all prophetic experiences in Scripture produce what happens to Elisha, but perhaps this is an example of what can happen (II Kings 8:11,12):

> *Then he set his countenance in a stare until he was ashamed; and the man of God wept. And Hazael said, "Why is my lord weeping?" And he answered, "Because I know the evil that you will do."*

As Elisha is receiving prophetic impressions, it may be by seeing things in what is sometimes called "the mind's eye" (though perhaps here it would be better to say the spirit's eye). This would account for the steady gaze or staring; he is looking past the visible realm into a revelation in the spiritual realm. A similar thing happens when Daniel is summoned to interpret Nebuchadnezzar's dream, (Daniel 4:19):

> *"Then Daniel, whose name was Belteshazzar, was astonished for a time, and his thoughts troubled him. So the king spoke,*

117

> *and said, 'Belteshazzar, do not let the dream or its*
> *interpretation trouble you.'"*

The shocking things Daniel perceives prophetically leave him for a time in a kind of solemn stupor.

Elisha may be seeing the violence that Hazael will do in the future. This would account for the weeping. It would seem that the experience of prophetic anointing can trigger powerful emotional feelings—weeping among them.

Prophetic process

An interesting insight into the prophetic process is revealed as one of the sons of the prophets, sent by Elisha, gives the word of the Lord to Jehu when he anoints him to be king of Israel. Elisha gives instructions to the man (II Kings 9:3):

> *"Then take the flask of oil, and pour it on his head, and say,*
> *Thus says the LORD: "I have anointed you king over*
> *Israel."" Then open the door and flee, and do not delay."*

What is interesting is how the prophetic message from the mouth of Elisha is enlarged in the mouth of the messenger. When this son of the prophets meets Jehu and pours the oil on his head, he begins approximately as Elisha told him (v. 6),

> *"Thus says the LORD God of Israel: 'I have anointed you*
> *king over the people of the LORD, over Israel."*

But then, instead of fleeing immediately, the man continues (v. 7-10),

> *"'You shall strike down the house of Ahab your master, that I*
> *may avenge the blood of My servants the prophets, and the*
> *blood of all the servants of the LORD, at the hand of Jezebel.*
> *For the whole house of Ahab shall perish... the dogs shall eat*
> *Jezebel in the vicinity of Jezreel, and there shall be none to bury*
> *her.'" And he opened the door and fled.*

There are several possible explanations for this enlarged message. One is that the man is making up the extra words out of his enthusiasm and basically creates a pious fraud that sounds impressive, but that is without authority. Or it is possible that verse 3 gives only the gist of Elisha's instructions, whereas he actually instructs the man with the complete message. Another possibility is that this is essentially the word that Elijah gives Ahab years previously about the miserable end of his reign, mentioned in I Kings 21:19-24. Perhaps the content of this message has been passed along and become known to the sons of the prophets.

But there is another possibility worth discussing. If prophecy is a supernatural utterance directed by the Holy Spirit and empowered by His anointing, then the delivery of the message is not necessarily something worked out ahead of time, but something that can be formed in the process of speaking it. As the man begins to speak the anointed words given to him by Elisha, he finds more words rising from his spirit and flowing out of his mouth. If this is true, then it might be the sort of thing Jesus describes when He tells His disciples that they will be persecuted and brought to trial (Matthew 10:19,20):

> "But when they deliver you up, do not worry about how or what you will speak. For it will be given to you in that hour what you should speak; for it is not you who speak, but the Spirit of your Father who speaks in you."

Prophecy is sometimes thought to be equivalent to preaching, but while preaching may in some cases be prophetic, this kind of message is clearly different from prepared sermons. The spontaneity of this process is not without its difficulties, as Paul points out (I Corinthians 14:29-32):

> Let two or three prophets speak, and let the others judge. But if anything is revealed to another who sits by, let the first keep silent. For you can all prophesy one by one, that all may learn and all may be encouraged. And the spirits of the prophets are subject to the prophets.

Perhaps the Corinthians were getting so many prophetic messages that they had not learned how to take turns in order properly to help the listeners. And so the apostle gives some practical advice about cooperating with the Holy Spirit.

When Paul says, "If anything is revealed to another who sits by, let the first keep silent," it would seem that, first of all, revelation is what prophecy is about. Without suggesting that New Testament prophets and prophecy are exactly like Old Testament Elisha and the sons of the prophets working with him, there may be this in common: that the prophetic message is not from a rational human source so much as from the Holy Spirit in a supernatural revelation of truth.

It might also be that when the prophetic anointing is flowing in one prophet, another, being influenced by that flow, can also begin to experience revelation.

Also, when Paul adds, "The spirits of the prophets are subject to the prophets," he seems to be saying that the prophetic experience is not weirdly ecstatic—a rush of words that cannot be controlled. Although it is revelation from the Holy Spirit, it is not without the voluntary cooperation of the human spirit.

What this may mean for the son of the prophets delivering a prophetic message to Jehu is that he begins with revelation given through Elisha's spirit, but he goes on to cooperate with the Holy Spirit in a further revelation given through his own spirit. This shared prophetic anointing—stirred up first in one and then affecting others—seems characteristic of the anointing in general. It is easier to sense a flow of the anointing once begun, and one person can share the flow with others. A suggestion might be to begin with what you have—whether your own or another person's anointing—and more may come.

Prophetic action

As an elder prophet sick with his final illness, Elisha receives a royal visitor. King Joash of Israel (II Kings 13:14)

> came down to him, and wept over his face, and said, "O my father, my father, the chariots of Israel and their horsemen!"

This reminds us of Elisha's own words when Elijah leaves him, being caught up in a whirlwind into the presence of God. It is likely that Joash has heard the story, and—perhaps partly to express his grief and partly to encourage Elisha—he hints at heaven. By talking like this, the king aligns with the unseen realm and opens himself up to a prophetic encounter with Elisha (vv. 15,16):

> *And Elisha said to him, "Take a bow and some arrows." So he took himself a bow and some arrows. Then he said to the king of Israel, "Put your hand on the bow." So he put his hand on it, and Elisha put his hands on the king's hands. And he said, "Open the east window"; and he opened it. Then Elisha said, "Shoot!" And he shot.*

These actions precede the prophetic words that follow, but the actions themselves are part of the message from God; the prophecy includes the action of taking up a bow and arrows, and also includes the placing of the prophet's hands on the king's hands.

Both Old and New Testaments contain other examples of prophetic actions.

King Saul, without knowing, performs a prophetic act by seizing Samuel's robe in desperation when Samuel tells him he is rejected as king. When the robe tears, Samuel says that the tear signifies the kingdom torn from Saul (I Samuel 15:27,28). Isaiah walks naked and barefoot for three years as a sign that Egypt will be led away naked and barefoot as captives of Assyria (Isaiah 20:2-4). Jeremiah buries a linen waistband until it rots to show the worthlessness of Judah in their stubbornness (Jeremiah 13:1-11). Hosea marries a prostitute whose unfaithfulness pictures the unfaithfulness of Israel (Hosea 1:2).

The elderly Zacharias doubts the angel Gabriel who tells him of the coming birth of John the Baptist, and is told by the angel that as a sign he will be mute until the birth of his son (Luke 1:18-20). Mary, sister of Lazarus and Martha, anoints Jesus with costly ointment while He is at dinner in Bethany. He says that this is for His burial (Mark 14:3-8 and John 12:3-7). Agabus, a prophet at Ceasarea, takes Paul's belt and binds his own feet and hands to show that Paul will be arrested and bound at Jerusalem (Acts

121

21:11).

In each of these cases, the Holy Spirit prompts people to act out a prophetic message. The anointing flows through a person's spirit and comes out as an action with a meaning. Why does God sometimes use prophetic actions to reveal and establish His purposes? Perhaps it is because there is a level of communication that is better acted out and viewed, rather than simply spoken.

With body language, we find many ways to express feelings and intentions. Likewise, facial expressions convey a variety of messages without the need for words. As we often say, "One picture is worth a thousand words." Stage and cinematic drama not only entertain; they speak to the soul in ways that go beyond words, as the actors move about and gesture.

Sometimes children in Sunday school are taught by means of an object lesson. Ordinary materials are used to illustrate spiritual truth—such as the illustration for the power of sinful habits I remember from my childhood. The teacher used a volunteer, whose wrists were tied by a single thread; on cue, the volunteer broke the thread easily. But next the thread was applied as a double strand. Breaking it was a little harder. Three and then four strands were tied in succession, until finally the volunteer could not break free at all. The object lesson taught my young heart an unforgettable warning: habits are hard to break.

And God sometimes uses prophetic object lessons. What is important to see is that actions can be a part of the prophetic process. We should look for prophetic object lessons in others, as well as expect them sometimes to be shown through ourselves.

Prophetic people

This may be a good place to discuss the prophetic expectation of the people of God. Although I offer here lessons in the anointing from the life of Elisha, an Old Testament prophet, I am writing for a New Testament audience. Among the various differences between the old covenant and the new is the level of prophetic involvement of God's people. Before Pentecost, which is one of the events transitioning from the old to the new covenant, prophecies come almost exclusively through a select group of prophets. That is why, for example, there is great surprise when Saul is met by a group of prophets (I Samuel 10:10,11):

> *Then the Spirit of God came upon him, and he prophesied among them. And it happened, when all who knew him formerly saw that he indeed prophesied among the prophets, that the people said to one another, "What is this that has come upon the son of Kish? Is Saul also among the prophets?"*

It wasn't usual for ordinary people to prophesy. When Joshua and another man are concerned that the Spirit of God rests unexpectedly upon Eldad and Medad who begin to prophesy, Moses says (Numbers 11:29),

> *"Oh, that all the LORD'S people were prophets and that the LORD would put His Spirit upon them!"*

Partly, this shows Moses' gentle godliness. But it also shows how rare prophetic activity is in the Old Testament.

In the New Testament we have a change—predicted in the book of Joel and begun at Pentecost—defined when Peter speaks to the crowd gathered to witness the phenomena that happen to the 120 believers after the onrush of the Holy Spirit. Peter explains (Acts 2:16-18),

> *"This is what was spoken by the prophet Joel: 'And it shall come to pass in the last days,' says God, 'that I will pour out of My Spirit on all flesh; your sons and your daughters shall prophesy…and on My menservants and on My maidservants I will pour out My Spirit in those days; and they shall prophesy.'"*

Among the things that characterize the pouring out of the Holy Spirit at Pentecost is that the people of God become a prophetic people. That is, the anointing tends to impart not just power in general, but the specific power of supernatural communication. What is unusual in the Old Testament—because it is unusual for the Holy Spirit to be poured out—becomes commonplace in the

123

New Testament, when the Holy Spirit has now been poured out for all who will receive Him.

Paul teaches (I Corinthians 14:31),

You can all prophesy one by one.

So it would seem that Paul expects believers in general to be prophetic. How do believers prophesy? What does it look and sound like? The usual way is likely to speak things from the mouth that are revealed in the spirit—impressions of God's purposes and of messages He wants people to know. These messages may not always consciously be given, and not always in a formal meeting of the church. For a simple example of speaking prophecy subconsciously, children are sometimes given names because they sound good to the parents, but long afterward it may be found that the meaning of a name matches the personality or life circumstances of a child. The naming, as it turns out, is prophetic.

But perhaps, like Elisha with Joash and the arrows, there are times when people will act out a message from the Lord. Again, it may be a conscious cooperation with the Holy Spirit as He releases a message through God's people. Or it may be an action, the significance of which appears only later.

I once asked a congregation to take a prophetic action. I had been preaching on a theme of repentance, and I asked people to stand who had something in their life that they were willing to repent of. Then I led them in a prayer of renunciation, after which I felt it would be useful to seal the prayer with an action. So I asked them to take a step from where they were standing to a different spot—forward, backward, or to either side, wherever there was room—as an action of faith that they were now in a new place of obedience and victory. I thought at the time that this action likely was prophetically inspired. But what amazed me was that less than a week later I was in another meeting with another preacher—who did exactly the same thing! I took encouragement from this repetition of what I had done (which, aside from these two times, I have never seen before nor since) that not only had I done the right—and effective—thing, but that God was using the second event to confirm my own prophetic sensitivity.

Sowing and reaping

As King Joash shoots the arrow out the window with Elisha's hands on his, the prophet says (II Kings 13:17),

> *"The arrow of the LORD's deliverance and the arrow of deliverance from Syria; for you must strike the Syrians at Aphek till you have destroyed them."*

This is the prophetic word that accompanies the prophetic action; together they complete the prophetic message. And it is more than a message; it is a verdict. The effectiveness of prophecy is not just in predicting the future, but in making the future happen. When God speaks—and this includes when God's Spirit speaks through men—an anointing is released to fulfill His purposes. True prophecies are more than inspiring words, they are tools of the spirit realm to bring about change. God says (Isaiah 55:10,11),

> *"For as the rain comes down, and the snow from heaven, and do not return there, but water the earth, and make it bring forth and bud, that it may give seed to the sower and bread to the eater, so shall My word be that goes forth from my mouth; it shall not return to Me void, but it shall accomplish what I please, and it shall prosper in the thing for which I sent it."*

Shooting the arrow and declaring the victory release the power.

But next Elisha says to Joash (II Kings 13:18),

> *"Take the arrows;" so he took them. And he said to the king of Israel, "Strike the ground"; so he struck three times, and stopped. And the man of God was angry with him, and said, "You should have struck five or six times; then you would have struck Syria till you had destroyed it. But now you shall strike Syria only three times."*

Whereas the first prophetic action—shooting an arrow out the window—seems almost unnecessary because it is followed by authoritative words, the second action carries all the weight of prophetic authority without any words.

125

We might want to sympathize with Joash when Elisha shows his anger. After all, how is he supposed to know that there is a direct connection between how many times he strikes the ground with the arrows and how many times he gains military victory in war with Syria? But since Elisha does get angry, we can assume that Joash should know. Perhaps what he should know is not so much about striking arrows on the ground in particular, but about how the anointing works in general. The rule he should know is always to use the anointing in abundance. When the Spirit is moving, it is time to move with Him without holding back.

Paul warns (II Corinthians 9:6),

> *But this I say: He who sows sparingly will also reap sparingly, and he who sows bountifully will also reap bountifully.*

Although Paul is speaking to the Corinthians specifically about financial giving, what he says sheds light on ministry in general. He goes on to say (vv.8-11),

> *And God is able to make all grace abound toward you, that you, always having all sufficiency in all things, have an abundance for every good work…. Now may He…supply and multiply the seed you have sown and increase the fruits of your righteousness, while you are enriched in everything for all liberality.*

When we act in the anointing two things happen: God gives us an abundant supply for the purpose at hand; and the results reflect that abundance. We are acting neither in isolation, nor from our own resource. We are engaging the supernatural power of God and we can therefore expect supernatural results.

The problem for Joash is that he is not operating in a supernatural frame of mind. Instead of acting with zeal, he is dutiful and reserved. As he strikes the ground with the arrows, he is doing just enough to obey, but not enough to enter into the anointed, prophetic moment.

There is such a thing as misplaced zeal. Paul says of religious Jews (Romans 10:2),

> *For I bear them witness that they have a zeal for God, but not according to knowledge.*

But enthusiasm for truth and the things of God is good. When Jesus casts the merchants and moneychangers out of the temple, because it is intended as a house of prayer, His disciples see a fulfillment of Psalm 69—David's own expression of zeal (John 2:17):

> *Then His disciples remembered that it was written, "Zeal for Your house has eaten Me up."*

A lack of fervent zeal disappoints and repulses the glorified Christ—who is at least as angry as Elisha with Joash—when He exposes the Laodiceans (Revelation 3:15,16):

> *"I know your works, that you are neither cold nor hot. I could wish you were cold or hot. So then, because you are lukewarm, and neither cold nor hot, I will spew you out of My mouth."*

Polite, well-balanced religion is offensive to God, who favors extremes instead. The Lord continues His rebuke of the Laodiceans (v. 19),

> *"As many as I love, I rebuke and chasten. Therefore be zealous and repent."*

God is looking for a zealous response from His people. And He commands repentance from mediocrity.

Fanatical faith and radical obedience are far more acceptable to heaven than to earth, and among men there is a stigma upon zealous people. Zeal is a nuisance and an embarrassment. Zeal is not the result of cool, deliberate thinking; it rises with a rush of excitement and confidence, and acts with an extravagance of energy. And usually ordinary people take a dim view of zealots because they don't fit in with ordinary life.

But it is the zealots who gain the greatest victory in the end, because they get excited about engaging the anointing. They are more interested in following the upward call than in following convention. They are willing to pay the price of looking ridiculous and being misfits to move in the power of God.

The anointing calls for boldness and authority. But Joash, too restrained for reckless cooperation with the anointing, taps out a timid response, and misses the invitation to overwhelming prophetic blessing. Perhaps he is protecting his dignity. Perhaps he is hiding behind a low-key personality. Perhaps he thinks prophetic enthusiasm is only for prophets. Whatever the excuse, the result is a victory of much less proportion than he might have had.

11

THE BONES

The anointing lives on

The final story takes place after Elisha's death (II Kings 13:20,21):

> *Then Elisha died, and they buried him. And the raiding bands from Moab invaded the land in the spring of the year. So it was, as they were burying a man, that suddenly they spied a band of raiders; and they put the man in the tomb of Elisha; and when the man was let down and touched the bones of Elisha, he revived and stood on his feet.*

At least two principles of the anointing can be seen in this strange account. The first is the fact that the anointing can attach to things and places. In general, this is one of the reasons we can describe the anointing as a substance. Apparently supernatural power remains upon the bones of the prophet and is released into the new corpse, bringing the man to life. It does make the story seem almost like a medieval tale of relics—bones of reputed saints supposed to have miraculous powers, displayed in shrines, and sought after, even today, by what some would say are gullible religious people. Although we can't dismiss the story of Elisha's bones—it is in the Bible after all—this sort of thing is not repeated anywhere else in Scripture, and so we cannot claim that it is something likely to happen in a literal way today—although we must allow the possibility.

Much more important, however, may be the simple and encouraging principle that the anointing outlives anointed people and continues to bring the dead to life. Godly influence and an open door for the anointing proceed from the life of those who live in faith, speaking to the hearts of others after them. From the very beginning of human history this has been true (Hebrews 11:4):

> By faith Abel offered to God a more excellent sacrifice than
> Cain, through which he obtained witness that he was righteous,
> God testifying of his gifts, and through it, he being dead still
> speaks.

One of the obvious ways that this can happen is through the writings by and about godly people—in and out of the Scriptures. Long after their decease, the sweet presence of God lingers in devotional writings of true saints, to be discovered and savored by generations following. Their names become household words in the household of God, their lives show us a pattern of godliness, and their stories pass on to us access to the anointing they enjoyed. Biographies and journals of great men and women of faith can influence readers with the same Holy Spirit who guided the writers.

Even when there are no biographies or journals published, leaving many godly men and women largely unknown, the anointing can touch their physical and spiritual descendents. The fire of God continues to burn—to smolder for a while, perhaps, and then to burst into a flame of spiritual awakening—although no one can remember the one who started the fire.

Sometimes the anointing touches hearts because of the prayers of faithful intercessors, long silenced by death, but whose anointed praying in their lifetime released the power of God to continue touching family members, communities, and entire nations.

Paul, writing of the death and resurrection of believers in Jesus, encourages us with these words (I Corinthians 15:58):

> Therefore, my beloved brethren, be steadfast, immovable,
> always abounding in the work of the Lord, knowing that your
> labor is not in vain in the Lord.

It is safe to say that whatever labor is "in the Lord" is anointed. And whatever is anointed will bear results, if not in our lifetime, then after we have gone on.

This book is really about touching the bones of Elisha. The career of this prophet, detailed as it is in Bible history, leaves us with a wonderful resource—lessons in the anointing that are timeless. But the thoughts written here are not intended merely to catalog a set of principles. My hope is that believing hearts, when exposed to the stories of the people of God living in the anointing and moving in power, can also experience that same power.

While it is said of Elijah rather than Elisha specifically that he (James 5:17)

was a man with a nature like ours,

it is important to see that this description also applies to Elisha, as well as to all of the other men and women of faith whose stories are in the Bible. What makes each of them remarkable is not that they are great in themselves, but that they have the anointing. Prophets who challenge nations and who write the Scriptures, warriors who do exploits, and women whose faith fulfills the will of God are ordinary people who find themselves carried in a flow of supernatural revelation and power quite beyond their natural ability. If their lives tell us anything it is that ordinary people are extraordinary when the Holy Spirit touches them.

Although our circumstances may differ from these ordinary people in the Bible, we share the source of power that makes them extraordinary. We do them no credit by placing them in a class above us, as though we could never live supernaturally.

Before us are the bones—the experiences of generations past touched by the anointing. We can investigate the bones, archeologist-style, carefully measuring and dating and speculating. We can write and read books about the lives of people long ago. We can become authorities on the history of how heaven touched earth and how the Spirit once moved.

It is a safe business—this digging in the dust. The battles fought, the invasions withstood, the plagues suffered, the kingdoms risen and fallen are all comfortably removed by the space of centuries and generations. As long as we keep it all textual and theoretical we also keep it removed from ourselves, and we never risk experiencing any of the things we study; none of it ever touches our heart. Much of church history is about the few who discover the anointing and live in its power, followed by the many who admire them from various distances. Often the first generation that follows an empowered life is blessed with the lingering flow of power. But in time the bones are buried and the power becomes a legend.

Jesus has some stern words for religious people who simply honor the memory of the prophets (Matthew 23:29-31):

> "Woe to you, scribes and Pharisees, hypocrites! Because you build the tombs of the prophets and adorn the monuments of the righteous, and say, 'If we had lived in the days of our fathers, we would not have been partakers with them in the blood of the prophets.' Therefore you are witnesses against yourselves that you are sons of those who murdered the prophets. Fill up, then, the measure of your fathers' guilt."

Jesus seems to be saying that one is no worse than the other; to kill anointed people is no worse than merely to honor their memory. The message of the prophets is not about attracting honor to themselves; it is about the power of God. And for us to fail to engage the power is equal to doing violence to the prophets. Honoring the bones is not the same as touching the bones. Revering the writings and telling of the exploits are among the means, but are in no way the end of a worthy pursuit. We need to discover more than the historical records about anointed people; we need to discover for ourselves the anointing that has blessed them.

One way to do this is to be more or less like the corpse in the story—dead. C. S. Lewis has pointed out, "Nothing that has not died can be resurrected," and if what we are seeking is a new flow of life, we might as well give up our pretensions to spiritual success in order to receive what we really need. The gospel is about redemption—and what can need redeeming more than lives lived without the power of God? In Psalm 23 the anointing on the head, and the overflowing of the cup, come only after a walk through the valley of the shadow of death.

In the closing chapters of *The Last Battle,* the final book in the Chronicles of Narnia series for children by C. S. Lewis, the present world comes to a cataclysmic end, even as a door is opened into a much more real world, and a call is heard, "Farther up and farther in!" While doubters huddle in their blindness, accusing others of deception, the faithful ones press on past the door to discover vistas, one after another, of such splendor as to thrill their hearts over and over with each new layer of reality. One character observes to another, "The farther up and the farther in you go, the bigger everything gets. The inside is larger than the outside."

Those who say that since they already have received assurance of salvation there is therefore nothing more for them to receive, will never, while they doubt, touch the bones of the anointed past. Nor will they accept any renewal of spirit from the lives and ministries of saints today who have dared to press into a supernatural grace. They will refuse to be thrown, helpless, into the place of death that they might be empowered with life.

But those who perceive that there is more of the power of God to experience—more of the anointing to receive—have a wonderful resource in the history of God's dealings with willing vessels. If they long to be touched by the anointing, they will read the stories of grace and of glory, of the power and of the Presence with humble eagerness. They will open their hearts to the Holy Spirit and say, "Come, Holy Spirit! Fill me! Pour Your anointing all over me! Breathe on me with the breath of heaven, so I can enjoy heaven on earth! Empower me with the fire of God, so I can empower others!"

They will seek out those whose experience in the anointing is transferable—like a holy virus. They will learn to take chances with God, allowing Him to set aside their own sense of what is reasonable and decorous, as they plunge into the river of God until they become childlike and free. They will expect the miracles and manifestations of a supernatural God. They will feast as at a banquet and clothe themselves in riches, and then run to share with others their discovery.

They will learn to endure the rejection and judgment of

those who do not see the invisible. They will disregard any cost because the chariots of fire all around are so much more real than the threats of enemies or the derision of friends. They will turn their backs on the old life and the old identity, and will take up the new mantle of the anointing with joyful faith, heeding the call resonating in their hearts to go *farther up and farther in!*

www.ingramcontent.com/pod-product-compliance
Lightning Source LLC
LaVergne TN
LVHW091152080426
835509LV00006B/647